Student Problem Manual

for use with

INVESTMENTS

Zvi Bodie
Boston University

Alex Kane
University of California, San Diego

Alan J. Marcus
Boston University

Manual prepared by
Richard E. Callaway
University of Tennessee

1989

IRWIN

Homewood, IL 60430
Boston, MA 02116

© Richard D. Irwin, Inc., 1989

All rights reserved. No part of this publication may be reproduced, stored in a retrieval system, or transmitted, in any form or by any means, electronic, mechanical, photocopying, recording, or otherwise, without the prior written permission of the publisher.

Printed in the United States of America.

ISBN 0-256-07498-4

5 6 7 8 9 0 P 6 5 4 3 2

This Study Guide is designed to supplement the material in Investments, by Bodie, Kane and Marcus. The study of investments requires that the student be proficient in a variety of quantitative techniques. It is the goal of this Study Guide to develop those skills in the student.

In addition to problems, the guide provides an outline and highlights of each chapter. These are intended to help the student organize topics from the chapter and to provide a brief summary of the important points of the chapter. It is hoped that these will better allow the student to see the interrelationships of topics throughout the book.

The major portion of the guide consists of problems designed to give the student practice with the quantitative techniques used in each chapter. By working these problems, the student should gain a clearer understanding of the mathematics used in the chapter. Whenever the material of the chapter overlaps material from the CFA exam, questions from past CFA exams are included. These problems should give the student a better feel for how the concepts of the text are employed.

                                        Richard E. Callaway
                                        The University of Tennessee at Chattanooga

Contents

	Prologue	1
1	The Investment Environment	2
2	Markets and Instruments	4
3	How Securities Are Traded	19
4	Concepts and Issues	28
5	Risk and Risk Aversion	38
6	Capital Allocation between the Risky Asset and the Risk-Free Asset	49
7	Optimal Risky Portfolios	59
8	The Capital Asset Pricing Model	72
9	Index Models	80
10	Arbitrage Pricing Theory	87
11	Equilibrium with Multiple Sources of Risk: The Multifactor CAPM	96
12	Empirical Evidence on Security Returns	101
13	Market Efficiency	104
14	Bond Prices and Yields	110
15	The Term Structure of Interest Rates	118
16	Fixed Income Portfolio Management	129
17	Equity Valuation	139
18	Fundamental Analysis	151
19	An Introduction to Options Markets	159
20	Options Markets: A Closer Look	171
21	Futures and Forward Markets: General Principles	186
22	Futures Markets: A Closer Look	194
23	The Theory of Active Portfolio Management	202
24	Portfolio Performance Evaluation	210
25	International and Extended Diversification	220
26	Organizational Structure and Management Issues	229
27	Principles of Portfolio Management	238
28	Individual Investors and Pension Funds	249

Prologue

OUTLINE

I. The risk-return tradeoff

II. Efficient diversification

III. Portfolio management

    A. Passive
    B. Active
        1. Market timing
        2. Security selection

IV. Equilibrium pricing relationships

HIGHLIGHTS

Investors will only bear more risk if they are compensated by higher expected returns. Modern Portfolio Theory shows that, on average, investors bear less risk when holding a portfolio of risky assets than if just one asset were held. Investors differ as to whether an active or passive portfolio management strategy is best. The Efficient Markets Hypothesis states that an active strategy involving market timing and security selection will not yield abnormal returns in the long run. However, without the resources dedicated to security analysis, the markets would cease to be efficient.

1 The Investment Environment

OUTLINE

I. Real assets vs. financial assets

II. Clients of the financial system

    A. Household sector

    B. Business sector

    C. Government sector

III. The environment responds

    A. Financial intermediation
        1. Mutual funds
        2. Investment banking

    B. Financial innovation
        1. Pass-throughs
        2. Primitive vs. derivative securities
        3. Response to taxation and regulation

IV. Markets and market structure

    A. Direct search

    B. Brokered
        1. Primary
        2. Secondary
        3. Block trades

    C. Dealer

    D. Auction

V. Recent trends

    A. Globalization

    B. Securitization

    C.   Credit enhancement

    D.   Bundling vs. unbundling

VI. Relationship between households and business

HIGHLIGHTS

Many different financial assets and markets have arisen to meet the needs of the clients of the financial system. Financial intermediaries exist to aid in the transfer of funds between those with funds to invest and those with a need for funds. Derivative securities offer clients risk-return combinations not available with primitive securities. As the financial system becomes more global in nature, more innovation in financial instruments is expected as investors' needs change.

2 Markets and Instruments

OUTLINE

I. Money Markets

    A. T-bills
        1. Bank discount yield
        2. Effective annual yield
        3. Bond equivalent yield

    B. Certificates of deposit

    C. Commercial paper

    D. Bankers acceptances

    E. Euro dollars

    F. Repos and reverses

    G. Federal funds

    H. Brokers calls

    I. The labor market

II. Capital markets

    A. T-notes and T-bonds
        1. Yield to maturity
        2. Yield to call

    B. Federal agency debt

    C. Municipal bonds
        1. Equivalent taxable yield
        2. Cutoff tax bracket

    D. Corporate bonds

    E. Mortgages and mortgage-backed securities

    F. Equity securities

          1. Common stock
          2. Preferred stock
          3. Mutual funds

    G. Stock market indices
          1. Price-weighted
          2. Market value-weighted
          3. Equally-weighted
          a. Arithmetic
          b. Geometric

    H. Bond market indicators

III. Derivative markets

    A. Options
          1. Call
          2. Put

    B. Futures contracts

HIGHLIGHTS

Securities are classified as either money market instruments or capital market instruments. The money markets consist of short-term, low-risk instruments while the capital markets consist of longer-term, riskier securities. The money markets are a subset of the bond market while the capital markets include equity instruments, bonds, and derivative securities such as options and futures. To gauge the performance of the markets both stock indices and bond indices are used. Corporate securities differ in the claim on income and assets that each security represents, and thus differ in risk. For a given corporation, bonds are the least risky, followed by preferred stock and then common stock. The major difference between an option contract and a futures contract is that one must perform on a futures contract, while one may choose not to exercise an option contract if the price of the underlying asset moves against one.

PROBLEMS

1. Consider a $10,000 par value T-bill with a 91-day maturity.
   a. What is the bank discount yield if the bill is sold for $9750?
   b. What is the bank discount yield if the bill is sold for $9900?
   c. What is the bank discount yield if the bill is sold for $9500?

2. Calculate the effective annual yield for the bills in Problem 1.

3. Calculate the bond equivalent yield for the bills in Problem 1.

4. What is the price of a 40-day, $10,000 face T-bill with a bank discount yield of
   a. 5.5%?
   b. 5.0%?
   c. 6.0%?

5. What is the price of a 30-day, $10,000 face T-bill with a bond equivalent yield of
   a. 6.0%?
   b. 6.5%?
   c. 5.5%?

6. Calculate the bid/ask spread in dollars for a 90-day, $10,000 face T-bill quoted in The Wall Street Journal with an ask of 6.24% and a bid of 6.32%.

7. Calculate the equivalent taxable yield for a municipal bond that yields 9% for investors with the following marginal tax rates:
   a. 20%
   b. 30%
   c. 40%

8. Determine the cutoff tax brackets for the following municipal yields, assuming the taxable yield is 10%.
   a. 4%
   b. 6%
   c. 8%

9. Calculate the yield ratios for the bonds in Problem 8.

10. Calculate the dividend yields for a stock that closed at $42.00 with the following annualized dividends:
    a. $1.00
    b. $1.50
    c. $2.50
    d. $4.00

11. Determine last year's earnings for the stock in Problem 10 given the following P/E ratios:
    a. 7
    b. 10
    c. 12
    d. 15

Use the following information for questions 12-15:

Base Year

Stock	Price	Shares
A	$40	10,000,000
B	$50	20,000,000
C	$60	30,000,000

Current Year

Stock	Price	Shares
A	$22	20,000,000
B	$55	20,000,000
C	$66	30,000,000

12. What is the percentage change in a price-weighted index?

13. What is the percentage change in a market value-weighted index?

14. What is the percentage change in an equally-weighted index?

15. What is the geometric average of the returns?

16. What is the profit or loss per share to an investor who bought a call option for $4 per share with an exercise price of $50 if the price of the stock at expiration is
    a. $40?
    b. $50?
    c. $60?
    d. $70?

17. What is the profit or loss per share to an investor who bought a put option for $3 per share with an exercise price of $60 if the price of the stock at expiration is
    a. $70?
    b. $60?
    c. $30?
    d. $ 0?

18. What is the profit to a trader who takes a long position in the S&P 500 futures at 250 and at expiration the S&P 500 is at
    a. 240?
    b. 250?
    c. 260?
    d. 270?

19. Answer Problem 18 assuming the trader takes a short position in the futures.

CFA PROBLEMS

20. (CFA Examination 1982, Level I) The variable that causes the equilibrium between the demand for and the supply of loanable funds is the
    a. money supply
    b. level of inflation
    c. change in real GNP
    d. interest rate

21. (CFA Examination 1987, Level I) A 120-day T-bill is priced at $9700 and has a discount yield of 9%. Its bond equivalent yield is
    a. 9%
    b. 9.12%
    c. 9.28%
    d. 9.41%

22. (CFA Examination 1987, Level I) A primary advantage of U.S. T-bonds is
    a. high liquidity
    b. low credit risk
    c. favorable state and local tax treatment
    d. all of the above

23. (CFA Examination 1982, Level I) Define real rate of interest.

24. (CFA Examination 1982, Level I) Why might you see a wide spread between the yield on treasuries and the yield on high grade corporate bonds?

25. (CFA Examination 1987, Level I) What is the Bey of a 90-day T-bill with a price of $9800?

26. (CFA Examination 1987, Level I) The bank discount yield of a 60-day T-bill is 8.5%. What is the BEY?

27. (CFA Examination 1985, Level I) The trustees of a large pension plan have asked you, as an investment manager, to provide some suggestions for investing in money-market securities. You have submitted the following issues:

Security	Yield
3-month T-bill	8.65%
3-month GMAC Commercial Paper	8.90%

3-month Citibank Bankers Acceptance   9.15%
3-month Citibank Domestic CD   9.25%

The trustees are curious as to why each security provides a different yield. They have asked you to give several illustrations explaining the differences in non-mathematical terms.

A. Briefly compare the important characteristics of the T-bill and the GMAC commercial paper that explain why the commercial paper provides a higher yield.

B. Briefly compare the important characteristics of the Citibank B/A with those of the Citibank CD that explain why the CD provides a higher yield.

SOLUTIONS

1. a. $\text{bdy} = \dfrac{250 \times \frac{360}{91}}{10{,}000} = 9.89\%$

   b. $\text{bdy} = \dfrac{100 \times \frac{360}{91}}{10{,}000} = 3.96\%$

   c. $\text{bdy} = \dfrac{500 \times \frac{360}{91}}{10{,}000} = 19.78\%$

2. a. $\dfrac{250}{9750} = .02564$

    eay $= (1 + .02564)^4 - 1 = 10.66\%$

　　b. $\dfrac{100}{9900} = .01010$

    eay $= (1 + .01010)^4 - 1 = 4.10\%$

　　c. $\dfrac{500}{9500} = .05263$

    eay $= (1 + .05263)^4 - 1 = 22.77\%$

3. a. bey $= \dfrac{250}{9750} \times \dfrac{365}{91} = 10.28\%$

　　b. bey $= \dfrac{100}{9900} \times \dfrac{365}{91} = 4.05\%$

　　c. bey $= \dfrac{500}{9500} \times \dfrac{365}{91} = 21.11\%$

4. a. P $= \$10{,}000 \times (1 - .055 \times \dfrac{40}{360}) = \$9938.89$

　　b. P $= \$10{,}000 \times (1 - .05 \times \dfrac{40}{360}) = \$9944.44$

　　c. P $= \$10{,}000 \times 1 - .06 \times \dfrac{40}{360} = \$9933.33$

5. a. P $= \dfrac{\$10{,}000}{1 + \dfrac{.06(30)}{365}} = \$9950.93$

　　b. P $= \dfrac{\$10{,}000}{1 + \dfrac{.065(30)}{365}} = \$9946.86$

　　c. P $= \dfrac{\$10{,}000}{1 + \dfrac{.055(30)}{365}} = \$9955.00$

6. Ask $= \dfrac{\$10{,}000}{1 + \dfrac{.0624(90)}{365}} = \$9848.47$

    Bid $= \dfrac{\$10{,}000}{1 + \dfrac{.0632(90)}{365}} = \$9846.56$

    Spread $= \$1.91$

7. a. ety $= \dfrac{.09}{1 - .2} = .11251$

b. $ety = \dfrac{.09}{1-.3} = .1286$

c. $ety = \dfrac{.09}{1-.4} = .15$

8. a. cutoff tax bracket = $1 - \dfrac{.04}{.10} = 60\%$

b. cutoff tax bracket = $1 - \dfrac{.06}{.10} = 40\%$

c. cutoff tax bracket = $1 - \dfrac{.08}{.10} = 20\%$

9. a. .4
b. .6
c. .8

10. a. dividend yield = $\dfrac{1}{42} = 2.38\%$

b. $dy = \dfrac{1.50}{42} = 3.57\%$

c. $dy = \dfrac{2.50}{42} = 5.95\%$

d. $dy = \dfrac{4}{42} = 9.52\%$

11. a. $eps = \dfrac{\$42}{7} = \$6.00$

b. $eps = \dfrac{\$42}{10} = \$4.20$

c. $eps = \dfrac{\$42}{12} = \$3.50$

d. $eps = \dfrac{\$42}{15} = \$2.80$

12. Initial value = $\dfrac{40 + 50 + 60}{3} = 50$

new value of divisor $\dfrac{20 + 55 + 66}{x} = 50$

$x = 2.6$

current value = $\dfrac{22 + 55 + 66}{2.6} = 5$

The value of the index increased 10%.

13. Initial value of the index = 100

current value = $\dfrac{22(20) + 55(20) + 66(30)}{40(10) + 50(20) + 60(30)} \times 100 = 110$

The value of the index increased 10%.

14. Initial value of index = 100
    Investing $2400 in each of the stocks, the equally weighted portfolio consists of 60 shares of A, 48 shares of B, and 49 shares of C.

    current value =

    $\dfrac{22(120) + 55(48) + 66(40)}{40(60) + 50(48) + 60(40)} \times 100 = 110$

    The value of the index increased 10%.

15. 10%

16. The value of the option at expiration is the maximum of (1) the stock price less the exercise price and (2) zero. The profit is the value of the option minus the purchase price.
    a. 0 - $4 = -$4
    b. 0 - $4 = -$4
    c. $10 - $4 = $6
    d. $20 - $4 = $16

17. The value of the option at expiration is the maximum of (1) the exercise price less the stock price and (2) zero. The profit is the value of the option minus the purchase price.
    a. 0 - $3 = -$3
    b. 0 - $3 = -$3
    c. $30 - $3 = $27
    d. $60 - $3 = $57

18. a. 240 - 250 = -10 x $500 = -$5000
    b. 250 - 250 = 0
    c. 260 - 250 = 10 x $500 = $5000
    d. 270 - 250 = 20 x $500 = $10,000

19. The short position is just the opposite of the long position.
    a. $5000
    b. 0
    c. -$5000
    d. -$10,000

20. d.

21. $bey = \dfrac{300}{9700} \times \dfrac{365}{120} = 9.41\%$

22. d.

23. The real rate of interest is the difference between nominal interest rates and some measure of inflation, such as the consumer price index or the GNP deflator. In other words, it is an inflation-adjusted interest rate.

24. The treasuries are more liquid and safer than the high-grade corporates. Also treasuries do not have the restrictive call provisions that corporates often have. The added risk to the investor results in higher yields to the corporate bonds.

25. $bey = \dfrac{200}{9800} \times \dfrac{365}{90} = 8.28\%$

26. $P = \$10,000 \, (1 - .085 \times 60/360) = \$9858.33$

    $bey = \dfrac{141.67}{9858.33} \times \dfrac{365}{60} = 8.74\%$

27. a. The GMAC has default risk where the T-bill has none. The T-bill is more liquid than the GMAC and receives favorable state and local tax treatment.

    b. The CD is backed only by Citibank and is unsecured. The B/A is guaranteed by Citibank, is guaranteed by the issuing bank, and is secured by the goods being financed. In addition, the market for the B/A is much more active than the market for the CD.

3 How Securities Are Traded

OUTLINE

I. The primary market

    A. Underwriting

    C. Underpricing

II. The secondary market

    A. Exchanges

    B. The over-the-counter market

    C. Third and fourth markets

III. Trading on exchanges

    A. Participants

        1. Commission brokers
        2. Floor brokers
        3. Registered traders
        4. Specialists

    B. Types of orders

        1. Market
        2. Limit
        3. Day
        4. Open
        5. Stop-loss
        6. Stop-buy

    C. Specialists and the execution of traders

IV. Trading on the OTC market

V. Margin transactions

        A. Initial margin

        B. Maintenance margin

        C. Margin or short sales

   VI. Regulation of securities markets

  XII. Mutual funds

        A. Closed-end vs. open-end

        B. Load vs. no-load

        C. Index

        D. Income

        E. Growth

        F. Unit investment trusts

        G. Commingled

        H. REIT

HIGHLIGHTS

   Securities are initially offered in the primary market where investment bankers typically assume the price risk of the issue. Trading in existing issues takes place in the secondary market, on centralized exchanges, or in the fragmented OTC market. Exchange specialists are charged with maintaining a fair and orderly market and have an information monopoly in the form of the limit order book. Investors can increase the possible returns and risks associated with an investment by buying on margin. The SEC regulates the equity markets with the goal of keeping a level playing field for all investors. Mutual funds have differing objectives, but all offer the investor the opportunity to hold a diversified portfolio for a much smaller investment than if the investor were to buy shares in the individual companies himself.

PROBLEMS

1. You have $10,000 which you invest for one year in XYZ stock, which is currently selling for $50 per share. You cannot purchase on margin.
    a. How many shares can you purchase?

    b. What is the return if the stock price at the end of the year is $70?

2. What is the profit from the investment in Problem 1?

3. Answer Problem 1 assuming you can purchase on margin with a 50% initial margin and your broker charges 9% on borrowed funds.

4. What is the profit from the investment in Problem 3?

5. What is your return if you invest, not on margin, $3000 in ABC stock at $30/share and one year later sell it for $33/share?

6. Answer Problem 5 assuming you purchase on margin. There is a 50% initial margin and your broker charges 8% on borrowed funds.

7. You have $25,000 which you invest for one year in AOK stock, which is currently selling for $10. You cannot purchase on margin.
   a. How many shares can you purchase?
   b. What is the return if the stock price is $7 at the end of the year?

8. What is the profit from the investment in Problem 7?

9. Answer Problem 7 assuming you can purchase on margin with a 50% initial margin and your broker charges 10% on borrowed funds.

10. What is the profit from the investment in Problem 9?

11. What is your return if you invest, not on margin, $5000 in DEF stock at $25/share and one year later it is selling for $20/share?

12. Answer Problem 11 assuming you purchase on margin. There is a 50% initial margin and your broker charges 9% on borrowed funds.

13. Assume you purchase $10,000 worth of GHI stock at $40/share. You invest $5000 and borrow $5000. At what price will you violate the maintenance margin if it is
    a. 45%?
    b. 40%?
    c. 35%?
    d. 30%?

14. Answer Problem 13 assuming the purchase price is $50/share.

15. You feel JKL stock will decline in the future so you sell short 4000 shares at $50/share. There is a 50% initial margin. At what price will you violate the maintenance margin if the margin is
    a. 40%?
    b. 35%?

c. 30%?
   d. 25%?

SOLUTIONS

1. a. $\dfrac{10000}{50} = 200$ shares

   b. $\dfrac{70-50}{50} = 40\%$

2. profit = ending value - beginning value
   profit = $14,000 - $10,000 = $4000

3. a. There is a 50% initial margin so borrow $10,000 and purchase 400 shares.

   b. $\text{return} = \dfrac{(28,000 - 10,000 - 900) - 10,000}{10,000}$

   $= \dfrac{7100}{10,000} = 71\%$

4. profit = ending value of stock - what is owed to broker - initial investment
   profit = $28,000 - $10,900 - $10,000 = $7100

5. $\dfrac{33-30}{30} = 10\%$

6. Investing $3000 of your own and borrowing $3000, the return is

   $\dfrac{(6600 - 3000 - 240) - 3000}{3000} = 12\%$

7. a. $\dfrac{25,000}{10} = 2500$ shares

   $\dfrac{7-10}{10} = -30\%$

8. $7(2500) - \$25,000 = -\$7500$

9. a. 5000 shares

   b. $$\text{return} = \frac{[7(5000) - 25,000 - 2500] - 25,000}{25,000}$$

   return = −70%

10. $7(5000) - \$27,500 - \$25,000 = -\$17,500$

11. $\frac{20 - 25}{25} = -20\%$

12. Investing $5000 of your own and borrowing $5000, the return is

    $$\frac{(8000 - 5000 - 450) - 5000}{5000} = -49\%$$

13. a. $\frac{250\,P - 5000}{250\,P} = .45$

    $137.5\,P = 5000$
    $P = \$36.36$

    b. $\frac{250\,P - 5000}{250\,P} = .4$

    $150\,P = 5000$
    $P = \$33.33$

    c. $\frac{250\,P - 5000}{250\,P} = .35$

    $162.5\,P = 5000$
    $P = \$30.77$

    d. $\frac{250\,P - 5000}{250\,P} = .3$

    $175\,P = 5000$
    $P = 28.57$

14. a. $\frac{200\,P - 5000}{200\,P} = .45$

    $P = \$45.45$

    b. $\frac{200\,P - 5000}{200\,P} = .4$

    $P = \$41.67$

c. $\dfrac{200P - 5000}{200P} = .35$

  P = $38.46

d. $\dfrac{200P - 5000}{200P} = .3$

  P = $35.71

15. a. $\dfrac{300{,}000 - 4000P}{4000P} = .4$

  5600 P = 300,000
  P = $53.57

b. $\dfrac{300{,}000 - 4000P}{4000P} = .35$

  5400 P = 300,000
  P = $55.56

c. $\dfrac{300{,}000 - 4000P}{4000P} = .3$

  5200 P = 300,000
  P = $57.69

d. $\dfrac{300{,}000 - 4000P}{4000P} = .25$

  5000 P = 300,000
  P = 60

4 Concepts and Issues

OUTLINE

I. Determinants of the level of interest rates

    A. Real rate of interest

    B. Inflation

    C. Risk premium

II. Holding period return

    A. Capital gains yield

    B. Dividend yield

III. Risk

IV. The historical record

V. Risk in the portfolio context

VI. The law of one price

VII. Continuous compounding

HIGHLIGHTS

The expected rate of return on any investment is the sum of the real rate of interest, the expected rate of inflation, and a premium based on the risk of the investment. The risk of a portfolio is measured by the standard deviation of return on the portfolio. The risk of a security is the risk that it contributes to the investor's total portfolio. The proposed positive relationship between expected return and risk is confirmed by historical holding period returns. The law of one price states that assets or groups of assets with the same distribution of returns must sell for the same price. This no risk-free arbitrage condition establishes pricing relationships across markets and across securities.

PROBLEMS

1. Given the following nominal yields on one-year risk-free securities, calculate the expected rate of inflation using the exact method. The real rate of interest is 4%.
   a. 5%
   b. 8%
   c. 16%

2. Answer Problem 1 assuming the real rate of interest is 3%.

3. Answer Problem 2, but now use the approximation.

4. Using the approximation, determine the nominal yields on the following securities. The real rate of interest is 5%.

Security	Expected Inflation	Risk Premium
A	2%	4%
B	2%	5%
C	3%	8%
D	4%	8%

5. Answer Problem 4 assuming the real rate of interest is 6%.

6. Using the approximation, what is the real rate of interest if expected inflation is 4% and the nominal yield on a security is 16%? The risk premium associated with the security is 7%.

7. A risk-free zero-coupon bond with ten years to maturity has a face value of $500 and sells for $192.77.
    a. What is the nominal yield on the bond?
    b. What is the real yield on the bond if the inflation rate over the life of the bond is 5%?

c. What is the real yield if the inflation rate is 8%?

8. A $1000 face, zero-coupon, risk-free bond with five years to maturity sells for $542.76.
   a. What is the nominal yield on the bond?
   b. What is the real yield on the bond if the inflation rate over the life of the bond is 7%?
   c. What is the real yield on the bond if the inflation rate is 13%?

9. What is the price of a $1000 face, zero-coupon, risk-free bond with eight years to maturity if the expected inflation rate is 2% and the real rate of interest is 5%?

10. Calculate the dividend yield, capital gains, yield, and holding period return for each of the following securities:

Security	Beginning price	Ending Price	Dividend
A	$100	$105	$4.00
B	$ 30	$ 33	$1.50
C	$ 40	$ 41	$2.40

Use the following information for Problems 11-14:

State of the Economy	Probability	Holding Period Returns A	B	C
recession	.2	-5%	-20%	15%
normal	.5	8%	10%	10%
upturn	.3	15%	40%	7%

11. Calculate the expected return and standard deviation of return for security A.

12. Calculate the expected return and standard deviation of return for security B.

13. Calculate the expected return and standard deviation of return for security C.

14. Stock B sells for $50 and Stock c sells for $100. The stocks pay no dividends. Calculate the expected return and standard deviation of return for an equally weighted portfolio of B and C.

15. If you deposit $1000 into an account that pays 5% interest compounded continuously, what will be the value of the account in four years?

16. What is the price of a $1000 face value, zero-coupon bond that matures in ten years if the interest rate is 8% compounded continuously?

SOLUTIONS

1. a. expected inflation = $\frac{1.05}{1.04} - 1 = .96\%$

   b. $\frac{1.08}{1.04} - 1 = 3.85\%$

   c. $\frac{1.16}{1.04} - 1 = 11.54\%$

2. b. $\frac{1.08}{1.03} - 1 = 4.85\%$

   c. $\frac{1.16}{1.03} - 1 = 12.62\%$

3. a. 5% - 3% = 2%
   b. 8% - 3% = 5%
   c. 16% - 3% = 13%

4. nominal yield on A = 5% + 2% + 4% = 11%
   nominal yield on B = 5% + 2% + 5% = 12%
   nominal yield on C = 5% + 3% + 8% = 16%
   nominal yield on D = 5% + 4% + 8% = 17%

5. All yields increase by one percentage point.

6. 16% - 7% - 4% = 5% real interest rate.

7. a. $192.77 (1 + r)^{10} = 500$
   $r = .10$ or 10%

b. real yield = $\frac{1.10}{1.05} - 1 = 4.76\%$

c. $\frac{1.10}{1.08} - 1 = 1.85\%$

8. a. $542.76 (1 + r)^5 = 1000$
   $r = .13$ or 13%

   b. $\frac{1.13}{1.07} - 1 = 5.61\%$

   c. zero

9. nominal rate = 7% by approximation, 7.1% by exact method

   $$P^2 = 1000/(1.07)^8 = \$582.01$$
   $$1000/(1.071)^8 = \$577.68$$

10. dividend yield$_A$ = $\frac{4}{100}$ = 4%

    dividend yield$_B$ = $\frac{1.50}{30}$ = 5%

    dividend yield$_C$ = $\frac{2.40}{40}$ = 6%

    capital gains$_A$ = $\frac{5}{100}$ = 5%

    capital gains$_B$ = $\frac{3}{30}$ = 10%

    capital gains$_C$ = $\frac{1}{40}$ = 2.5%

    HPR$_A$ = 4% + 5% = 9%
    HPR$_B$ = 5% + 10% = 15%
    HPR$_C$ = 6% + 2.5% = 8.5%

11. $E(R) = .2(-.05) + .5(.08) + .3(.15) = .075$ or 7.5%

   std dev $= [.2(-.05 -.075)^2 + .5(.08 -.075)^2 + .3(.15 -.075)^2]^{.5}$

   $= [.2(.015625) + .5(.000025) + .3(.005625)]^{.5}$

   $= (.004825)^{.5}$
   $= .06946$ or 6.946%

12. $E(R) = .2(-.2) + .5(.10) + .3(.40) = .13$ or 13%

   std dev $= [.2(-.2 -.13)^2 + .5(.1 -.13)^2 + 3(.4 -.13)^2]^{.5}$

   $= [.2(.1089) + .5(.0009) + .3(.0729)]^{.5}$

   $= (.0441)^{.5}$
   $= .21$ or 21%

13. $E(R) = .2(-.15) + .5(.10) + .3(.07) = .041$ or 4.1%

   std dev $= [.2(-.15 -.401)^2 + .5(.10 -.401)^2 + .3(.07 -.401)^2]^{.5}$

   $= [.2(.036481) + .5(.003481) + .3(.000841)]^{.5}$

   $= (.009289)^{.5}$
   $= .09638$ or 9.638%

14. Converting returns to prices

State of Economy	Probility	Price of B	Price of C
recession	.2	$40	$115
normal	.5	$55	$110
upturn	.3	$70	$107

    invest $200 to buy two shares of B and one share of C

State	Value of Portfolio	Return
recession	$195	-2.5%
normal	$220	10%
upturn	$247	23.5%

    $E(R) = .2(-.025) + .5(.10) + .3(.235) = .1155$ or 11.55%

    std dev $= [.2(-.025 -.1155)^2 + .5(.10 -.1155)^2 + .3(.235 -.1155)^2]^{.5}$

    $= [.2(.01974025) + .5(.00024025) + .3(.01428025)]^{.5}$

$$= (.00835225)^{.5}$$
$$= .09139 \text{ or } 9.139\%$$

15. future value = $1000\ e^{.05(4)}$ = $1221.40

16. present value = $1000/e^{.08(10)}$ = $449.33

5 Risk and Risk Aversion

OUTLINE

I. Risk and risk aversion
   A. Risk with simple prospects
   B. Risk premium
   C. Speculation vs. gambling

II. Utility values
   A. Risk aversion, risk neutrality, risk loving
   B. Certainty equivalent rate
   C. Mean-variance criterion

III. Portfolio risk
   A. Asset risk vs. portfolio risk
      1. Hedging
      2. Diversification
   B. Portfolio mathematics
      1. Mean and variance
      2. Covariance and correlation

IV. Appendix A: A defense of mean-variance analysis
   A. Describing probability distributions
   B. Fundamental approximation theorem
   C. Normal and lognormal distributions

V. Appendix B: Risk aversion and expected utility

HIGHLIGHTS

Risk exists whenever the payoff to an investment is uncertain; whenever more than one outcome is possible. Investors are assumed to be risk-averse, meaning they will turn down a fair gamble. Risk-averse investors require a risk premium in order to make a risky investment. The size of the premium is based on the riskiness of the investment.

The fundamental approximation theorem shows that the mean and variance of return to a portfolio are equally important in choosing the optimal portfolio, and that higher moments may be ignored. The covariance, and thus the correlation, of an individual asset's returns with the portfolio's returns determine whether the asset will reduce the risk of the portfolio, and, if so, by how much. The assumption of the normality of stock returns is shown to be a good assumption over short periods of time.

PROBLEMS

1. You currently have total wealth of $50,000. You may invest your wealth in T-bills at 6% or invest in a risky prospect that will double your money or halve it with equal probability.
   a. What is your expected wealth if you take the risky investment?
   b. What is your expected wealth if you take the risk-free investment?
   c. What is the risk premium of the risky investment in terms of wealth?
   d. What is the variance of wealth of the risky asset?
   e. What is the variance of wealth of the risk-free asset?

2. Answer Problem 1 in terms of returns rather than wealth.

3. Calculate the expected return, standard deviation of return, and risk premium of the following investment. The T-bill rate is 10%.

State of Nature	Probability	Return
recession	.25	-20%
normal	.5	15%
boom	.25	40%

4. At what T-bill rate would no risk-averse investor take the risky investment in Problem 3?

5. At what T-bill rate would no investors take the risky investment in Problem 3?

6. Which of the following investments will be accepted by an investor whose utility function is given by equation 5.1 and who has A = 4? The T-bill rate is 10%.

Investment	Expected Return	Standard deviation
A	.28	.20
B	.29	.25
C	.30	.30
D	.33	.40

7. Answer Problem 6 for A = 2.

8. Answer Problem 6 for A = 6.

Use the following information for Problems 9-12:

State	Probability	Return on A	Return on B	Return on C
recession	.3	.05	-.10	.10
normal	.4	.10	.10	.08
boom	.3	.15	.30	.06

9. a. Calculate the expected return and variance of return for each of the assets.

    b. Which of the assets does not satisfy the mean-variance criterion?

10. Calculate the covariance of each pair of assets.

11. Calculate the correlation coefficient of each pair of assets.

12. Calculate the expected return and variance of a portfolio combining assets A and C that places
    a. 20% of the wealth in A
    b. 40% of the wealth in A
    c. 60% of the wealth in A
    d. 80% of the wealth in A

Use the following information for Problems 13-17:

State	Probability	Return on x	Return on y	Return on z
recession	.1	.14	.06	-.06
downturn	.2	.12	.08	.06
normal	.4	.10	.10	.12
upturn	.2	.08	.12	.18
boom	.1	.06	.14	.30

13. Calculate the expected return and variance of return for each of the assets.

14. Calculate the covariance of each pair of assets.

15. Calculate the correlation coefficient of each pair of assets.

16. Calculate the expected return and variance of an equally weighted portfolio of
    a. x and y
    b. x and z
    c. y and z

17. Calculate the expected return and variance of a portfolio of x and y that places
    a. 40% of the wealth in x
    b. 60% of the wealth in x
    c. 80% of the wealth in x

SOLUTIONS

1. a. E(w) = .5($100,000) + .5($25,000) = $62,500
    b. E(w) = $50,000 (1.06) = $53,000
    c. $62,500 - $53,000 = $9,500
    d. variance = $.5(\$100,000 - \$62,500)^2 + .5(\$25,000 - \$62,500)^2$
        = 703,125,000 + 703,125,000
        = 1,406,250,000
    e. zero

2. a. E(r) = .5(1) + .5(-.5) = .25
    b. E(r) = .06
    c. .25 - .06 = .19
    d. variance = $.5(1 -.25)^2 + .5(-.5 -.25)^2$
        = .28125 + .28125
        = .5625
    e. zero

3. E(r) = .25(-.2) + .5(.15) + .25(.4) = .125

    var = $.25(-.2 -.125)^2 + .5(.15 -.125)^2 + .25(.4 -.125)^2$
        = .02640625 + .0003125 + .01890625
        = .045625

    std dev = $(.045625)^{.5}$ = .2136
    risk premium = .125 - .10 = .025

4. If the T-bill rate were .125, no risk-averse investor would hold the risky asset as he would earn the same expected return risklessly with the T-bill.

5. If the T-bill rate were above .4, not even a risk-seeking investor would hold this asset.

6. U(A) = $.28 - 2(.2)^2$ = .2

    U(B) = $.29 - 2(.25)^2$ = .165

    U(C) = $.30 - 2(.3)^2$ = .12

    U(D) = $.33 - 2(.4)^2$ = .01

    The utility of the risk-free asset is .10 so the investor would choose all but D.

7. U(A) = $.28 - (.2)^2$ = .24

$U(B) = .29 - (.25)^2 = .2275$

$U(C) = .30 - (.3)^2 = .21$

$U(D) = .33 - (.4)^2 = .17$

All the investments are acceptable.

8. $U(A) = .28 - 3(.2)^2 = .16$

   $U(B) = .29 - 3(.25)^2 = .1025$

   $U(C) = .30 - 3(.3)^2 = .03$

   $U(D) = .33 - 3(.4)^2 = -.15$

   Only A and B are acceptable.

9. a. $E(r_A) = .3(.05) + .4(.10) + .3(.15) = .10$

   $\begin{aligned}Var_A &= .3(.05 - .10)^2 + .4(.10 - .10)^2 + .3(.15 - .10)^2 \\ &= .3(.0025) + 0 + .3(.0025) \\ &= .0015\end{aligned}$

   $E(r_B) = .3(-.10) + .4(.10) + .3(.30) = .10$

   $\begin{aligned}Var_B &= .3(-.10 - .10)^2 + .4(.10 - .10)^2 + .3(.30 - .10)^2 \\ &= .3(.04) + 0 + .3(.04) \\ &= .024\end{aligned}$

   $E(r_C) = .3(.10) + .4(.08) + .3(.06) = .08$

   $\begin{aligned}Var_C &= .3(.10 - .08)^2 + .4(.08 - .08)^2 + .3(.06 - .08)^2 \\ &= .3(.0004) + 0 + .3(.0004) \\ &= .00024\end{aligned}$

   b. B

10. $Cov_{AB} = .3(-.05)(-.2) + 0 + .3(.05)(.2)$

    $= .006$

    $Cov_{AC} = .3(-.05)(.02) + 0 + .3(.05)(-.02)$

    $= -.0006$

    $Cov_{BC} = .3(-.2)(.02) + 0 + .3(.2)(-.02)$

    $= -.0024$

11. $Corr_{AB} = .006/[(.0015)^{.5}(.024)^{.5}] = 1$

$$\text{Corr}_{AC} = -.0006/[(.0015)^{.5}(.00024)^{.5}] = -1$$

$$\text{Corr}_{BC} \; -.0024/[(.024)^{.5}(.00024)^{.5}] = -1$$

12. a. $E(r) = .2(.10) + .8(.08) = .084$

    $\text{Var} = .2^2(.0015) + .8^2(.00024) + 2(.2)(.8)(-.0006)$
    $= .00006 + .0001536 - .000192$
    $= .0000216$

    b. $E(r) = .4(.10) + .6(.08) = .088$

    $\text{Var} = .4^2(.0015) + .6^2(.00024) + 2(.4)(.6)(-.0006)$
    $= .00024 + .0000864 - .000288$
    $= .0000384$

    c. $E(r) = .6(.10) + .4(.08) = .092$

    $\text{Var} = .6^2(.0015) + .4^2(.00024) + 2(.6)(.4)(-.0006)$
    $= .00054 + .0000384 - .000288$
    $= .0002904$

    d. $E(r) = .8(.10) + .2(.08) = .096$

    $\text{Var} = .8^2(.0015) + .2^2(.00024) + 2(.8)(.2)(-.0006)$
    $= .00096 + .0000096 - .000192$
    $= .0007776$

13. $E(r_x) = .1(.14) + .2(.12) + .4(.10) + .2(.08) + .1(.06) = .10$

    $\text{Var}_x = .1(.04)^2 + .2(.02)^2 + .4(0) + .2(-.02)^2 + .1(-.04)^2$
    $= .00016 + .00008 + 0 + .00008 + .00016$
    $= .00048$

    $E(r_y) = .1(.06) + .2(.08) + .4(.10) + .2(.12) + .1(.14) = .10$

    $\text{Var} = .1(-.04)^2 + .2(-.02)^2 + 0 + .2(.02)^2 + .1(.04)^2$
    $= .00016 + .00008 + 0 + .00008 + .00016$
    $= .00048$

    $E(r_z) = .1(-.06) + .2(.06) + .4(.12) + .2(.18) + .1(.30) = .12$

    $\text{Var}_z = .1(-.18)^2 + .2(-.06)^2 + 0 + .2(.06)^2 + .1(.18)^2$
    $= .00324 + .00072 + 0 + .00072 + .00324$
    $= .00792$

14. $\text{cov}_{xy} = .1(.04)(-.04) + .2(.02)(-.02) + 0$
    $+ .2(-.02)(.02) + .1(-.04)(.04)$
    $= -.00016 - .00008 + 0 - .00008 - .00016$
    $= -.00048$

$$\text{cov}_{xz} = .1(.04)(-.18) + .2(.02)(-.06) + 0$$
$$+ .2(-.02)(.06) + .1(-.04)(.18)$$
$$= -.00072 - .000241 + 0 - .00024 - .00072$$
$$= -.00192$$

$$\text{cov}_{yz} = .1(-.04)(-.18) + .2(-.02)(-.06) + 0$$
$$+ .2(.02)(.06) + .1(.04)(.18)$$
$$= .00072 + .00024 + 0 + .00024 + .00072$$
$$= .00192$$

15. $\text{corr} = -.00048/[(.00048)^{.5}(.00048)^{.5}] = -1$

    $\text{corr} = -.00192/[(.00048)^{.5}(.00792)^{.5}] = -.985$

    $\text{corr} = .00192/[(.00048)^{.5}(.00792)^{.5}] = .985$

16. a. $E(r) = .5(.10) + .5(.10) = .10$

    $\text{Var} = .25(.00048) + .25(.00048) + .05(-.00048)$
    $= 0$

    b. $E(r) = .5(.10) + .5(.12) = .11$

    $\text{Var} = .25(.00048) + .25(.00792) + .5(-.00192)$
    $= .00012 + .00198 - .00096$
    $= .00114$

    c. $E(r) = .5(.10) + .5(.12) = .11$

    $\text{Var} = .25(.00048) + .25(.00792) + .5(.00192)$
    $= .00012 + .00192 + .00096$
    $= .003$

17. a. $E(r) = .-1(.10) + .6(.10) = .10$

    $\text{Var} = .4^2(.00048) + .6^2(.00048) + 2(.4)(.6)(-.00048)$
    $= .0000768 + .0001728 - .0002304$
    $= .0000192$

    b. Same as a.

    c. $E(r) = .10$

    $\text{Var} = .8^2(.00048) + .2^2(.00048) + 2(.8)(.2)(-.00048)$
    $= .0003072 + .0000192 - .0001536$
    $= .0001728$

6 Capital Allocation Between the Risky Asset and the Risk-Free Asset

OUTLINE

I. Risk reduction with the risk-free asset

II. The risk-free asset

III. Portfolios of one risk-free asset and one risky asset

　　A. The Capital Asset Line

　　B. The reward-to-variability ratio

　　C. Differential borrowing and lending rates

IV. Risk tolerance and asset allocation

V. Passive investment strategy

HIGHLIGHTS

The risk of the investor's complete portfolio can be reduced by transferring funds from the risky asset to the risk-free asset, or the risk can be increased by transferring funds from the risk-free asset to the risky asset. If the borrowing and lending rates are identical, combinations of the risk-free asset and the risky asset offer a constant reward-to-variability ratio; for each additional unit of risk taken on, the expected return rises by a constant amount. Investors choose the optimal mix of the risk-free and risky assets based on their tolerance for risk.

The more risk-tolerant the investor, the greater is the percentage of his complete portfolio invested in the risky asset. A passive investment strategy makes no attempt to identify the optimal risky asset, using instead a broad portfolio of risky assets intended to mimic the total market's movements.

PROBLEMS

1. The risk-free rate is 6%. The risky asset offers an expected return of 15%. Calculate the expected return on a portfolio of the

two assets with the following percentages invested in the risky asset:
a. 20%
b. 40%
c. 60%
d. 80%

2. What is the standard deviation for each of the portfolios in Problem 1 if the risky asset has a standard deviation of 9%?

3. What is the reward-to-variability ratio for each of the portfolios in Problem 2?

4. The risky asset offers an expected return of 15% and the risk-free rate is 8%. Calculate the expected return on a portfolio of the two assets with the following percentages invested in the risky asset:
a. 20%

b. 40%
   c. 60%
   d. 80%

5. If the risky asset has a standard deviation of 9%, what is the standard deviation of each of the portfolios in Problem 4?

6. What is the reward-to-variability ratio for each of the portfolios in Problem 5?

7. What is the reward-to-variability ratio for each of the portfolios in Problem 4 if the risky asset has a standard deviation of 6%?

8. Consider a risky portfolio that consists of 50% A, 30% B, and 20% C. What percentage does each of these assets make up of the complete portfolio of the risky asset and the risk-free asset, if the following percentages are invested in the risk-free asset?
   a. 10%
   b. 35%
   c. 60%
   d. 90%

9. Calculate the dollars invested in each of the individual assets in Problem 8, parts a and b, if a total of $500,000 is invested in the complete portfolio.

10. If the T-bill rate is 8% and the risky portfolio offers an expected return of 20% and has a standard deviation of 16%, what are the expected returns on the portfolios with the following standard deviations?
    a. 4%
    b. 8%
    c. 12%

11. Using the information in Problem 10, calculate the standard deviations of the portfolios with the following expected returns:
    a. 12%
    b. 16%
    c. 18%

12. If the risky asset offers an expected return of 22% and a standard deviation of 15%, what are the expected returns on the portfolios with the following standard deviations? The T-bill rate is 7%.
    a. 3%
    b. 6%
    c. 10%

13. Using the information in Problem 12, calculate the standard deviations of the portfolios with the following expected returns?
    a. 12%
    b. 16%
    c. 19%

14. Assume investors can borrow and lend at the risk-free rate of 10%. If the risky portfolio offers an expected return of 30% and a standard deviation of 25%, what is the expected return on the portfolios with the following percentages invested in the risky portfolio?
    a. 50%
    b. 90%
    c. 120%
    d. 200%

15. What is the standard deviation of each of the portfolios in Problem 14?

16. Answer Problem 14 assuming investors can lend at 10%, but must pay 12% to borrow.

17. Determine the optimal portfolios for investors with the following risk-aversion coefficients. The T-bill rate is 10% and the risky

asset offers a 25% expected return with a standard deviation of 18%.
a. 4
b. 6
c. 8
d. 10

18. Answer Problem 17 assuming the risky asset offers a 20% expected return.

SOLUTIONS

1. a. E(r) = .8(.06) + .2(.15) = .078
   b. E(r) = .6(.06) + .4(.15) = .096
   c. E(r) = .4(.06) + .6(.15) = .114
   d. E(r) = .2(.06) + .8(.15) = .132

2. a. Var = .2(.09) = .018
   b. Var = .4(.09) = .036
   c. Var = .6(.09) = .054
   d. Var = .8(.09) = .072

3. Choosing a portfolio at random:

   $$\frac{(.078 - .06)}{.018} = 1$$

4. a. E(r) = .8(.08) + .2(.15) = .094
   b. E(r) = .6(.08) + .4(.15) = .108

c. $E(r) = .4(.08) + .6(.15) = .122$
d. $E(r) = .2(.08) + .8(.15) = .136$

5. The standard deviations are the same as in Problem 2.

6. Choosing a portfolio at random

$$\frac{(.094 - .08)}{.018} = .778$$

7. Choosing a portfolio at random.

$Var = .2(.06) = .012$

$$\frac{(.094 - .08)}{.012} = 1.167$$

8. a. A: $.5(.9) = .45$ or 45%
      B: $.3(.9) = .27$ or 27%
      C: $.2(.9) = .18$ or 18%

   b. A. $.5(.65) = .325$
      B. $.3(.65) = .195$
      C: $.2(.65) = .13$

   c. A: $.5(.4) = .2$
      B: $.3(.4) = .12$
      C: $.2(.4) = .08$

   d. A: $.5(.1) = .05$
      B: $.3(.1) = .03$
      C: $.2(.1) = .02$

9. a. A: $.45(500,000) = \$225,000$
      B: $.27(500,000) = \$135,000$
      C. $.18(500,000) = \$\ 90,000$

   b. A: $.325(500,000) = \$162,500$
      B: $.195(500,000) = \$\ 97,500$
      C: $.13(500,000) = \$\ 65,000$

10. $y = $ std dev/std dev$_p$ $E(r) = r_f + y[E(r_p) - r_f]$

    a. $y = \frac{4}{16} = .25$

       $E(r) = .08 + .25(.12) = .11$

    b. $y = \frac{8}{16} = .5$

       $E(r) = .08 + .5(.12) = .14$

c. $y = \frac{12}{16} = .75$

$E(r) = .08 + .75(.12) = .19$

11. $y = \frac{E(r) - r_f}{E(r_p) - r_f}$ std dev $= y$ std dev$_p$

   a. $y = \frac{.04}{.12} = \frac{1}{3}$

   std dev $= 1/3(.16) = .0533$

   b. $y = \frac{.08}{.12} = \frac{2}{3}$

   std dev $= 2/3(.16) = .1067$

   c. $y = \frac{.10}{.12} = \frac{5}{6}$

   std dev $= 5/6 (.16) = .1333$

12. a. $y = \frac{.03}{.15} = .2$

   $E(r) = .07 + .2(.15) = .10$

   b. $y = \frac{.06}{.15} = .4$

   $E(r) = .07 + .4(.15) = .13$

   c. $y = \frac{.10}{.15} = \frac{2}{3}$

   $E(r) = .07 + 2/3(.15) = .17$

13. a. $y = \frac{.05}{.15} = \frac{1}{3}$

   std dev $= 1/3 (.15) = .05$

   b. $y = \frac{.09}{.15} = .6$

   std dev $= .6(.15) = .09$

   c. $y = \frac{.12}{.15} = .8$

   std dev $= .8(.15) = .12$

14. a. $E(r) = .5(.10) + .5(.30) = .20$
    b. $E(r) = .1(.10) + .9(.30) = .28$
    c. $E(r) = -.2(.10) + 1.2(.30) = .34$
    d. $E(r) = -1(.10) + 2(.30) = .50$

15. a. std dev $= .5(.25) = .125$
    b. std dev $= .9(.25) = .225$
    c. std dev $= 1.2(.25) = .30$
    d. std dev $= 2(.25) = .50$

16. a. .20 as the investor is in the lending portion of the CAL
    b. .28
    c. $E(r) = -.2(.12) + 1.2(.30) = .336$
    d. $E(r) = -1(.12) + 2(.30) = .48$

17. $y = [E(r_p) - r_f]/A\, Var_p$

    a. $y = \dfrac{.15}{4(.0324)} = 1.16$

    b. $y = \dfrac{.15}{6(.0324)} = .77$

    c. $y = \dfrac{.15}{8(.0324)} = .57$

    d. $y = \dfrac{.15}{10(.0324)} = .46$

18. a. $y = \dfrac{.10}{4(.0324)} = .77$

    b. $y = \dfrac{.10}{6(.0324)} = .51$

    c. $y = \dfrac{.10}{8(.0324)} = .39$

    d. $y = \dfrac{.10}{10(.0324)} = .31$

7 Optimal Risky Portfolios

OUTLINE

I. Diversification and portfolio risk

II. Portfolios of two risky assets

III. The optimal risky portfolio with a risk-free asset and two risky assets

    A. Determination of the optimal risky portfolio

    B. Determination of the optimal complete portfolio

IV. The Markowitz model

    A. Establishing the efficient frontier

    B. Determining the optimal risky portfolio

    C. Separation

V. Restrictions on the risk-free asset

    A. No risk-free asset

    B. No risk-free borrowing

    C. Different borrowing and lending rates

VI. Appendix A: The power of diversification

VII. Appendix B: Risk sharing vs risk pooling

VIII. Appendix C: The fallacy of time diversification

HIGHLIGHTS

By placing a small percentage of total wealth in each of a large number of risky assets, the investor can eliminate much of the risk associated with holding a single asset. The risk that may not be diversified away is known as market or systematic risk. The variance of a portfolio is largely determined by the covariance of the assets in the portfolio. The smaller the correlation coefficient, the more risk that may be eliminated. If two assets are perfectly negatively correlated, a riskless portfolio may be constructed from the assets. The efficient frontier consists of risky assets that offer the greatest expected return for a given risk level and the lowest risk for a given level of expected return. The optimal risky portfolio is the same for all investors if the risk-free borrowing and lending rates are equal. The optimal risky portfolio is obtained by maximizing the reward-to-variability ratio, which is done graphically by finding the ray from the risk-free rate that is tangent to the efficient frontier. The decision of which risky asset to invest in is separate from the decision of the proportions of the complete portfolio. Without equal borrowing and lending rates, a variety of risky portfolios will be chosen by different investors.

PROBLEMS

1. Given the following information, what are the weights of the minimum-variance portfolio?

	ABC		XYZ
E(r)	.20		.25
std dev	.40		.45
covariance		.108	

2. What are the expected return and standard deviation of the portfolio?

3. Answer Problem 1 assuming the covariance is -.081.

4. Answer Problem 2 assuming the covariance is -.081.

5. Given the following information, calculate the expected return on the zero-variance portfolio.

	DEF	GHI
E(r)	.13	.22
std dev	.25	.40
covariance	-.1	

6. Given the following information, calculate the expected return on the zero-variance portfolio.

	JKL	MNO
E(r)	.12	.18
std dev	.20	.30
covariance	-.06	

7. What is the risk-free rate in Problem 6?

   Use the following information for Problems 8-12:

	T-bills	Stock Fund 1	Stock Fund 2
E(r)	.08	.16	.18
std dev		.30	.35
covariance		.084	

8. What is the reward-to-variability ratio if fund 1 is used along with T-bills?

9. What is the reward-to-variability ratio if fund 2 is used?

10. Which portfolio gives the highest reward-to-variability ratio?

11. What is the expected return and standard deviation of the optimal risky portfolio?

12. What will be the percentages of each fund in the complete portfolio of an investor with A = 3?

Use the following information for Problems 13-18:

	T-bills	PQR	STU
E(r)	.06	.12	.18
std dev		.20	.45
covariance		-.054	

13. What is the slope of the CAL if PQR is used?

63

14. What is the slope of the CAL if STU is used?

15. What is the expected return and standard deviation of the optimal risky portfolio?

16. What is the slope of the optimal CAL?

17. What will be the percentages of each stock in the complete portfolio of an investor with A = 4?

18. Answer Problem 17 for A = 6.

CFA PROBLEMS

19. (CFA Examination 1986, Level I) Diversification can reduce portfolio risk only if security return correlation is:
    a. more than +1
    b. equal to +1
    c. less than +1
    d. zero

20. (CFA Examination 1986, Level I) Which portfolio cannot lie on the efficient frontier as described by Markowitz?

	Portfolio	Expected Return	Standard Deviation
a.	W	10%	20%
b.	X	5%	7%
c.	Y	15%	36%
d.	Z	12%	15%

21. CFA Examination 1987, Level I) You wish to estimate the correlation between the returns on stock A and stock B. Which set of information would you require?
    a. Expected return of stock A, expected return of stock B, beta of either stock A or stock B
    b. Beta of stock A, beta of stock B
    c. Beta of stock A, variance of stock B
    d. Covariance between stock A and stock B, standard deviation of stock A, standard deviation of stock B

22. (CFA Examination 1986, Level I) Portfolio theory is most concerned with:
    a. the elimination of systematic risk
    b. the effect of diversification on portfolio risk
    c. the identification of unsystematic risk
    d. active portfolio management to enhance returns

23. (CFA Examination 1987, Level I) Stocks A, B, and C each have same the expected return and standard deviation. Given the following

correlation matrix, which portfolio constructed from these stocks has the lowest risk?

Correlation Matrix

Stock	A	B	C
A	+1.0		
B	+0.8	+1.10	
C	+0.1	−0.3	+1.0

a. A portfolio equally invested in stocks A and B
b. A portfolio equally invested in stocks A and C
c. A portfolio equally invested in stocks B and C
d. A portfolio totally invested in stock C

24. (CFA Examination 1986, Level I) Which statement about portfolio diversification is correct?
   a. Proper diversification can reduce or eliminate systematic risk.
   b. The risk-reducing benefits of diversification do not occur meaningfully until at least 10 to 15 individual securities have been purchased.
   c. Because diversification reduces a portfolio's total risk, it necessarily reduces the portfolio's expected return.
   d. Typically, as more securities are added to a portfolio, total risk would be expected to fall at a decreasing rate.

25. (CFA Examination 1985, Level III) As director of research for a medium-sized investment firm, Jeff Cheney was concerned about the mediocre investment results experienced by the firm in recent years. He met with his two senior equity analysts to consider alternatives to the stock selection techniques employed in the past.

One of the analysts suggested that the current literature has examined the relationship between price/earnings ratios (P/E) and securities returns. A number of studies had concluded that high P/E stocks tended to have higher betas and lower risk-adjusted returns than stocks with low P/E ratios.

The analyst also referred to recent studies analyzing the relationship between security returns and company size as measured by equity capitalization. The studies concluded that when compared to the S&P 500 Index, small-capitalization stocks tended to provide above-average risk-adjusted returns while large-capitalization stocks tended to provide below-average risk-adjusted returns. It was further noted that little correlation was found to exist between a company's P/E ratio and the size of its equity capitalization.

Jeff's firm has employed a strategy of complete diversification and the use of beta as a measure of portfolio risk. He and his analysts were intrigued as to how these recent studies might be applied to their stock selection techniques and thereby improve their performance. Given the results of the studies indicated above:

a. Explain how the results of these studies might be used in the stock selection and portfolio management process. Briefly discuss the effects on the objectives of diversification and on the measurement of portfolio risk.

b. List and briefly discuss reasons why this firm might not want to adopt a new strategy based on these studies in place of its current strategy of complete diversification and the use of beta as a measure of portfolio risk.

SOLUTIONS

1. Using equation 7.7

$$W_{ABC} = \frac{.2025 - .108}{.16 + .2025 - .216} = \frac{.0945}{.1465} = .65$$

$$W_{XYZ} = 1 - .65 = .35$$

2. $E(r) = .65(.2) + .35(.25) = .2175$

   $\text{var} = .65^2(.16) + .35^2(.2025) + 2(.108)(.65)(.35)$
   $= .0676 + .02480625 + .04914$
   $= .14154625$

   std dev $= .37623$

3. $W_{ABC} = \frac{.2025 + .081}{.16 + .2025 + .162} = \frac{.2835}{.5245} = .54$

   $W_{GHI} = 1 - .54 = .46$

4. $E(r) = .54(.2) + .46(.25) = .223$

   $\text{var} = .54^2(.16) + .46^2(.2025) + 2(-.081)(.54)(.46)$
   $= .046656 + .042849 - .0402408$
   $= .0492642$

   std dev $= .22196$

5. $W_{DEF} = \frac{.4}{(.4 + .25)} = .62$

   $E(r) = .62(.13) + .38(.22) = .1642$

6. $W_{JKL} = \frac{.3}{(.2 + .3)} = .6$

   $E(r) = .6(.12) + .4(.18) = .144$

7. To prevent arbitrage, the risk-free rate must be .144.

8. $\frac{.08}{.3} = .2667$

9. $\frac{.10}{.35} = .2857$

10. Using equation 7.8

$$w_1 = \frac{(.16 - .08).1225 - (.18 - .08).084}{(.16 - .08).1225 + (.18 - .08).09 - (.16 - .08 + .18 - .08).084}$$

$$= \frac{.0098 - .0084}{.0098 + .009 - .01512}$$

$= .38$

$w_2 = 1 - .38 = .62$

11. $E(r) = .38(.16) + .62(.18) = .1724$

   $\text{var} = .38^2(.09) + .62^2(.1225) + 2(.38)(.62)(.084)$
   $= .012996 + .047089 + .0395808$
   $= .0996658$
   $\text{std dev} = .3157$

   reward-to-variability ratio $= \frac{.0924}{.3157} = .2927$

12. $y = \frac{.0924}{3(.0996658)} = .309$

   investment in fund 1 $= .309(.38) = .11742$
   investment in fund 2 $= .309(.62) = .19158$

13. $\frac{.06}{.2} = .3$

14. $\frac{.12}{.45} = .2667$

15. $W_{PQR} = \frac{.06(.2025) - .12(-.054)}{.06(.2025) + .12(.04) - (.18)(-.054)}$

   $= \frac{.01863}{.02667}$

   $= .70$

   $W_{stu} = 1 - .70 = .3$

   $E(r) = .7(.12) + .3(.18) = .138$

   $\text{var} = .7^2(.04) + .3^2(.2025) + 2(.7)(.3)(-.054)$
   $= .015145$
   $\text{std dev} = .12307$

16. $\frac{.1296}{.13745} = .943$

17. $y = \frac{.0696}{4(.0188928)} = .921$

>   investment in PQR = .921(.84) = .77364
>   investment in STU = .921(.16) = .14736

18. $y = \dfrac{.0696}{6(.0188928)} = .614$

    investment in PQR = .614(.84) = .51576
    investment in STU = .614(.16) = .09824

19. c

20. a

21. d

22. b

23. c

24. d

25. a. If the firm were to use the results of these studies to develop a new stock selection approach, it could probably weight the portfolio heavily with stocks having low P/E ratios and stocks of companies having small equity capitalization. Since little correlation was found to exist between a company's P/E ratio and its equity capitalization, a concentration of investment assets in companies having both attributes might maximize the risk-adjusted return of the portfolio.

    Since the approach just described favors concentration of portfolio assets in securities having specific attributes (low P/E ratios and small equity capitalization), the concept of "efficient" diversification in a capital asset pricing model context is not relevant. That is, unsystematic risk cannot be eliminated given the nature of the asset concentrations. However, prudence dictates that even an extreme application of this selection approach would require diversification in terms of the number of securities held and the industries within which the companies operate.

    The studies referred to in the question suggest that investors are compensated systematically for more than just the assumption of systematic risk. This makes beta an ineffective measure of risk. Additionally, since the selection approach may lead to less than "efficient" diversification, some risk measure other than beta is necessary. Total risk (the standard deviation of returns) is more appropriate.

    b. (1) There is strong empirical support indicating that the capital markets are semi-strong form efficient. If this is true, then the results of the studies cited in the exam question cannot be correct.

(2) Concentration of assets in stocks having two very similar attributes may expose the portfolio to more risk than is desirable.

(3) The strong theoretical and empirical support of capital market theory, if valid, would rule out inefficiency in the capital markets.

(4) The results of the studies cited in the examination question could be faulty due to methodological deficiencies, computational errors, or data collection errors.

(5) Even if the study results are correct as described, each such study covers a specific time period. There is no assurance that future time periods would yield similar results.

(6) In the extreme, adoption of the investment strategy implied by the studies could violate "prudent man" standards. (Specific asset purchases may be difficult to justify solely on the basis of low P/E ratios and small equity capitalization.)

(7) After the results of the studies became publicly known, investors could destroy the relationships that were formed. For example, if numerous investors identify and purchase stocks with low P/E ratios and small equity capitalization, the prices of these stocks will rise, increasing the P/E ratios. Each time the price of a stock with small equity capitalization begins to drop, investors will purchase it and prevent the P/E from ever reaching the "buy" level.

(8) The investment strategy implied by the studies may not be suitable for all investors. That is, the objectives of the individual may not be met by stocks with low P/E ratios and small equity capitalization.

8 The Capital Asset Pricing Model

OUTLINE

I. The standard capital asset pricing model (CAPM)

    A. Assumptions

    B. Implications

        1. All investors hold the market portfolio
        2. A passive strategy is efficient
        3. The Security Market Line

II. Extensions of the CAPM

    A. Zero-beta CAPM

    B. Different borrowing and lending rates

    C. Multi-period CAPM

HIGHLIGHTS

The CAPM relates the expected return on an asset to the risk of the asset. In the standard CAPM, investors follow the Markowitz model with risk-free borrowing and lending at the same rate, and all use the same expected returns, variances, and covariances in making their decisions. Thus, all investors see the same efficient frontier and, in maximizing the slope of the CAL, all hold the same risky portfolio, which is the market portfolio. The market portfolio consists of all assets, held in proportion to their market value. Separation, or the mutual fund theorem, applies as all investors can choose a passive strategy of investing in the risky mutual fund that is the market portfolio and T-bills. The risk of an asset is the risk it contributes to the market portfolio. Beta is a standardized measure of this risk, and the SML relates beta to expected return. The SML can be used to determine the expected return on an individual asset, while the CML can only be used for efficiently diversified portfolios. This is because the SML only prices that portion of the risk of an asset that remains in an efficiently diversified portfolio. The standard CAPM can be easily expanded to include different borrowing and lending rates as well as no risk-free asset. While the CAPM is a one-period model, if investor preferences and the distributions of security returns are stable, it is valid for multiple time periods.

PROBLEMS

1. What is the beta of a portfolio consisting of 25% A, 35% B, and 40% C?

	A	B	C
beta	1.2	.9	1.5

2. Using the information in Problem 1, calculate the expected return on an equally-weighted portfolio of the three securities. The risk-free rate = .08 and the expected return on the market = .17.

3. What is the expected return on a security with beta = .8 if the risk-free rate = .06 and the expected return on the market = .12?

4. Answer Problem 3 assuming expected inflation increases by .02.

5. Answer Problem 3 assuming the market risk premium doubles. Ignore the information in Problem 4.

6. What is the expected return on a security with beta = 1.5 if the risk-free rate = .08 and the market risk premium = .08?

7. Answer Problem 6 assuming expected inflation decreases by .03.

8. Answer Problem 6 assuming the market risk premium is halved. Ignore the information in Problem 7.

9. Answer Problem 6 assuming expected inflation decreases by .02 and the market risk premium doubles.

10. Determine the expected returns on the following securities if the risk-free rate = .07 and the market risk premium = .10.

	A	B	C
beta	.5	1.2	1.6

11. Answer Problem 10 assuming the risk-free rate falls to .05.

12. Answer Problem 10 assuming the market risk premium doubles. Ignore the information in Problem 11.

13. Given the risk-free rate = .06 and the expected return on the market = .14, identify each of the following securities as undervalued, overvalued, or correctly valued.

	X	Y	Z
beta	.5	1.2	1.4
analyst forecast of expected return	.12	.145	.172

14. Given the risk-free rate = .08 and the market risk premium = .10, identify each of the following securities as undervalued, overvalued, or correctly valued.

	D	E	G
beta	.8	.9	1.1
analyst forecast of expected return	.16	.17	.18

15. Using the following information, identify each of the following well-diversified portfolios as undervalued, overvalued, or correctly valued.

	H	I	J	MKT.	T-bills
variance	.03	.05	.06	.04	
analyst forecast of expected return	.125	.14	.22	.14	.08

16. If the zero-beta version of CAPM holds and the expected return on the zero-beta portfolio is .08 and the expected return on the market is .16, what are the expected returns on the following assets?

	G	H	I
beta	1.0	.5	1.5

CFA PROBLEMS

17. (CFA Examination 1986, level I) Which one of the following is not required in order to calculate a portfolio's expected rate of return using the Capital Asset Pricing Model?

    a. Expected return on the market
    b. Standard deviation of return
    c. Portfolio beta
    d. Risk-free rate

18. (CFA Examination 1986, Level I) What is the expected return of a zero-beta security?

   a. The market rate of return
   b. Zero rate of return
   c. A negative rate of return
   d. The risk-free rate of return

19. (CFA Examination 1986, Level I) Market risk can accurately be described by which one of the following statements?

   a. It is one important source of an investor's total variability of return.
   b. It causes price fluctuations which can be diversified away.
   c. It affects virtually all stocks in the same way and to the same degree.
   d. It is less important during rising as opposed to falling markets.

20. (CFA Examination 1986, Level I) Risk that cannot be diversified away is described as:

   a. specific
   b. extra-market
   c. systematic
   d. total

SOLUTIONS

1. beta = $.25(1.2) + .35(.9) + .4(1.5) = 1.215$
2. beta = $1/3(1.2) + 1/3(.9) + 1/3(1.5) = 1.2$
   $E(r) = .08 + 1.2(.17 - .08) = .188$
3. $E(r) = .06 + .8(.12 - .06) = .108$
4. $E(r) = .04 + .8(.10 - .04) = .088$
5. $E(r) = .06 + .8(.18 - .06) = .156$
6. $E(r) = .08 + 1.5(.08) = .20$
7. $E(r) = .05 + 1.5(.08) = .17$
8. $E(r) = .08 + 1.5(.04) = .14$
9. $E(r) = .06 + 1.5(.16) = .30$

10. $E(r_A) = .07 + .5(.10) = .12$

    $E(r_B) = .07 + 1.2(.10) = .19$

    $E(r_C) = .07 + 1.6(.10) = .23$

11. $E(r_A) = .05 + .5(.10) = .10$

    $E(r_B) = .05 + 1.2(.10) = .17$

    $E(r_C) = .05 + 1.6(.10) = .21$

12. $E(r_A) = .07 + .5(.20) = .17$

$E(r_B) = .07 + 1.2(.20) = .31$

$E(r_C) = .07 + 1.6(.20) = .39$

13. from the SML

$E(r_X) = .06 + .5(.08) = .10$

$E(r_Y) = .06 + 1.2(.08) = .156$

$E(r_Z) = .06 + 1.4(.08) = .172$

Comparing to the analyst forecast, we find Z is correctly valued, Y is overvalued (price must fall to raise expected return), and X is undervalued.

14. from the SML

$E(r_O) = .08 + .8(.10) = .16$

$E(r_E) = .08 + .9(.10) = .17$

$E(r_b) = .08 + 1.1(.10) = .19$

Comparing to the analyst forecast, D and E are correctly valued and G is overvalued.

15. from the CML

$E(r_H) = .08 + (.03/.04)(.06) = .125$

$E(r_I) = .08 + (.05/.04)(.06) = .155$

$E(r_J) = .08 + (.06/.04)(.06) = .17$

Comparing to the analyst forecast, H is correctly valued, I is overvalued, and I is undervalued

16. $E(r_G) = .08 + 1(.08) = .16.$

$E(r_H) = .08 + .5(.08) = .12$

$E(r_I) = .08 + 1.5(.08) = .20$

17. b
18. d
19. a
20. c

9 Index Models

OUTLINE

I. The single-index model

    A. Systematic vs. firm-specific risk

    B. Estimating the model

    C. Diversification

    D. CAPM and the single-index model

        1. Actual vs. expected returns
        2. The index model and the expected return-beta relationship

II. Implementing the single-index model

    A. The industry version

    B. Predicting beta

HIGHLIGHTS

The CAPM posits a relationship between beta and expected return. Expected returns are not observable, nor is the market portfolio and thus beta. Therefore, the CAPM is not implementable. The single-index models use realized returns on securities and an index portfolio that serves as a proxy for the market portfolio to estimate beta. Betas estimated in this manner change over time and exhibit a tendency to regress toward one. For this reason, the betas are adjusted by practitioners when using the single-index model.

PROBLEMS

1. The index model is estimated for stocks A and B with the following results. What is the variance of each stock and the covariance between them?

$R_A = .02 + .9 R_M + e_A$

$R_B = .01 + .8 R_M + e_B$

$\text{var}(R_M) = .09$

$\text{var}(e_A) = .16$

$\text{var}(e_B) = .04$

2. For the stocks in Problem 1, calculate the variance of a portfolio that is 60% A and 40% B. What is the nonsystematic portion of the variance?

3. The following results are from the estimation of the single-index model for stocks C and D. Calculate the variance of each stock and the covariance between them.

$R_C = .01 + .8 R_M + e_C$

$R_D = .03 + .5 R_M + e_D$

$\text{var}(R_M) = .16$

$\text{var}(e_C) = .09$

$\text{var}(e_D) = .04$

4. For the stocks in Problem 2, calculate the nonsystematic variance of a portfolio that is 75% C and 25% D.

Use the following information for Problems 5-7. The information is drawn from a three-stock capital market, and the index model holds.

Stock	Capitalization	Beta	Mean Excess Return	Standard Deviation
A	$5000	1.2	.096	.40
B	$3000	.9	.072	.30
C	$2000	.65	.052	.20

The standard deviation of the index is .25.

5. What is the mean excess return of the index portfolio?

6. What is the covariance between stock A and the index?

7. Answer Problem 6 for stock B.

8. What is the firm-specific component of the variance of stock A?

9. Answer Problem 8 for stock C.

Use the following information for Problems 10-13. The index model for stocks J and K is estimated with the following results:

$R_J = .01 + .75 R_M + e_A$

$R_K = .03 + 1.1 R_M + e_B$

$\text{var}(R_M) = .04 \qquad R^2_J = .20 \qquad R^2_K = .35$

10. What is the variance of each stock?

11. Determine the systematic and firm-specific components of the variance of each stock.

12. What is the covariance between each stock and the market index?

13. What is the correlation coefficient between the two stocks?

14. Given the following unadjusted betas, calculate the Merrill Lynch adjusted beta.
    a. 1.5
    b. .9
    c. 1.2

15. Using $beta_t = .2 + .9\ beta_{t-1}$, predict next year's unadjusted betas using the data in Problem 14.

SOLUTIONS

1. $\text{var}(R_A) = .9^2(.09) + .16 = .2329$

   $\text{var}(R_B) = .8^2(.09) + .04 = .0976$

   $\text{cov}_{AB} = .9(.8)(.09) = .0648$

2. $\text{var}(R_p) = .6^2(.2329) + .4^2(.0976) + 2(.6)(.4)(.0648) = .130564$

   beta of portfolio = $.6(.9) + .4(.8) = .86$

   systematic component = $.86^2(.09) = .066564$

   nonsystematic component = $.130564 - .066564 = .064$

3. $\text{var}(R_C) = .8^2(.16) + .09 = .1924$

   $\text{var}(R_D) = .5^2(.16) + .04 = .08$

   $\text{cov}_{CD} = .8(.5)(.16) = .064$

4. $\text{var}(R_p) = .75^2(.1924) + .25^2(.08) + 2(.75)(.25)(.064) = .137225$

   beta of portfolio = $.75(.8) + .25(.5) = .725$

   systematic variance = $.725^2(.16) = .0841$

   nonsystematic variance = $.137225 - .0841 = .053125$

5. the index portfolio has beta = 1, so the mean excess return is .08.

6. $\text{cov} = 1.2(.25)^2 = .075$

7. $\text{cov} = .9(.25)^2 = .05625$

8. total variance = .16

   systematic component = $(1.2)^2(.25)^2 = .09$

   firm-specific component = $.16 - .09 = .07$

9. total variance = .04

   systematic component = $(.65)^2(.25)^2 = .02640625$

   firm-specific component = $.04 - .02640625 = .01359375$

10. $\text{var} = B^2 \text{var}(Rm)/R^2$

$\text{var}(R_J) = .75^2(.04)/.2 = .1125$

$\text{var}(R_K) = (1.1)^2 (.04)/.35 = .138285714$

11. Stock K - systematic component = $(.75)^2(.04) = .0225$

    nonsystematic component = $.1125 - .0225 = .09$

    Stock J - systematic component = $(1.1)^2 (.04) = .0484$

    nonsystematic component = $.138285714 - .0484 = .089885714$

12. $\text{cov}(R_J, R_m) = .75(.04) = .03$

    $\text{cov}(R_K, R_m) = 1.1(.04) = .044$

13. $\text{cov}(R_J, R_K) = .75(1.1)(.04) = .033$

    $\text{corr}(R_J, R_K) = .033/[(.1125)^{.5}(.138285714)^{.5}]$
    $= .265$

14. a. adj. beta = $2/3(1.5) + 1/3 = 1.333$

    b. adj. beta = $2/3(.9) + 1/3 = .9333$

    c. adj. beta = $2/3(1.2) + 1/3 = 1.133$

15. a. beta = $.2 + .9(1.5) = 1.55$

    b. beta = $.2 + .9(.9) = 1.01$

    c. beta = $.2 + .9(1.2) = 1.28$

10 Arbitrage Pricing Theory

OUTLINE

I. Arbitrage

    A. Law of one price

    B. Dominant assets

    C. Risk-free vs. risky arbitrage

II. Arbitrage Pricing Theory

    A. Importance of well-diversified portfolios

    B. Betas and expected returns

    C. Individual assets and APT

    D. APT vs. CAPM

    E. Multifactor APT

HIGHLIGHTS

Arbitrage Pricing Theory relies on the simple condition of no risk-free arbitrage to formulate asset prices. Risk-free arbitrage results in a sure profit with no investment, so that any investor who discovers a violation of the no-arbitrage condition would assume an infinitely large position in the assets, and end the violation. APT relies on well-diversified portfolios to eliminate firm-specific risk, so that, as in CAPM, only systematic risk is priced. The single-factor APT results in the same asset pricing equation as CAPM, but without the restrictive assumptions. APT also allows for more than one source of systematic risk. This is an advantage over CAPM as many researchers find that more than one factor impacts security returns. Unfortunately, APT offers no insight as to which factors are important in pricing securities.

PROBLEMS

1. Assuming a one-factor APT model holds, calculate the expected returns on the well-diversified portfolios with the following betas. E(Rm) = .14 and the risk-free rate = .06.
   a. 0
   b. .5
   c. 1
   d. 1.5

2. Answer Problem 1 assuming the betas are for individual securities.

3. Assuming a one-factor APT model holds, calculate the expected returns on the following securities. The risk-free rate = .08 and the factor risk premium = .10.
   a. .8
   b. 1.2
   c. 1.4

4. Assuming a two-factor APT model holds, calculate the expected returns on the following securities. The risk-free rate = .05, the risk premium on the first factor = .06, and the risk premium on the second factor = .08.

   a. $beta_1 = 0$, $beta_2 = 1$

   b. $beta_1 = 1$, $beta_2 = 0$

   c. $beta_1 = .5$, $beta_2 = .5$

   d. $beta_1 = 1$, $beta_2 = 1$

5. Assuming a two-factor APT model holds, what are the expected returns on the following securities? The risk-free rate = .07, the risk-premium on the first factor = .08, and the risk premium on the second factor = .04.

   a. $beta_1 = .4$, $beta_2 = .4$

   b. $beta_1 = .4$, $beta_2 = 1.2$

   c. $beta_1 = .6$, $beta_2 = .8$

   d. $beta_1 = .9$, $beta_2 = 1.1$

6. Assuming a three-factor APT model holds, calculate the expected returns on the following securities. The risk-free rate = .04 and the factor risk premia are .06, .04, and .08 for factors one, two, and three, respectively.

a. $\beta_1 = .8$, $\beta_2 = .4$, $\beta_3 = .6$

b. $\beta_1 = 1.2$, $\beta_2 = .8$, $\beta_3 = .2$

c. $\beta_1 = 1.3$, $\beta_2 = .9$, $\beta_3 = .3$

7. Assuming a three-factor APT model holds, what are the expected returns on the following securities? The risk-free rate = .08 and the risk premia are .10, .04, and .06 for factors one, two and three, respectively.

    a. $\beta_1 = 2$, $\beta_2 = 1$, $\beta_3 = 1$

    b. $\beta_1 = .5$, $\beta_2 = .5$, $\beta_3 = .5$

    c. $\beta_1 = 0$, $\beta_2 = 1$, $\beta_3 = .5$

8. Assuming a one-factor APT model holds, what is the risk premium associated with the factor? What is the risk-free rate?

Security	E(R)	Beta
A	.20	1.3
B	.12	.5

9. Assuming a two-factor APT model holds, what are the risk premia associated with the factors? What is the risk-free rate?

Security	E(R)	Beta$_1$	Beta$_2$
A	.104	.4	.5
B	.208	.8	1.5
C	.128	.8	.5

10. Consider the following investment opportunities

Stock	Return in State 1	Return in State 2	Return in State 3
A	-.10	.07	.26
B	.20	.09	-.02
C	.04	.06	.08

Does an arbitrage opportunity exist? Consider an equally weighted portfolio of A and B.

11. For the stocks in Problem 10, if they all sell for $10/share, what is the minimum profit from shorting 100,000 shares of C and purchasing the portfolio?

12. How far must the price of stock C fall to eliminate the arbitrage possibility? Assume the dollar payoffs to C are unchanged.

Consider the following investment opportunities for Problems 13-15.

Stock	Return in State 1	Return in State 2	Return in State 3
D	-.06	.08	.25
E	.10	.09	.08
F	.30	.12	-.05

13. An arbitrage opportunity exists using an equally weighted portfolio of two of the stocks. What are the returns to this portfolio?

14. If all the stocks in Problem 13 sell for $20/share, what is the minimum profit from performing arbitrage and shorting 500,000 shares?

15. How much must the price of the dominated asset fall before

arbitrage is eliminated?

CFA Problems

16. (CFA Examination 1987, Level I) Arbitrage Pricing Theory (APT), when compared to the capital asset pricing model (CAPM), can be viewed most accurately as a:

    a. mutually exclusive but equally defensible theory.
    b. mathematically equivalent theory when applied to risk-averse investors.
    c. more general theory, which reduces to the CAPM under certain assumptions.
    d. controversial theory, which contradicts the basic tenets of the CAPM.

17. (CFA Examination 1986, Level II) Assume the return-generating process is described by two factors, A and B, and that the constant component of return is zero. A's factor value is .04 while B's factor value is -.12. XYZ Corporation's factor loading on A is 1.0 while its factor loading on B is 0.7. XYZ Corporation's total return is .06. Calculate XYZ Corporation's idiosyncratic (nonsystematic) return.

Solutions

1. a. $E(r) = .06 + .0(.08) = .06$

b. $E(r) = .06 + .5(.08) = .10$
c. $E(r) = .06 + 1(.08) = .14$
d. $E(r) = .06 + 1.5(.08) = .18$

2. The answers don't change as APT prices only systematic risk.

3. A. $E(r) = .08 + .8(.10) = .16$
   b. $E(r) = .08 + 1.2(.10) = .20$
   c. $E(r) = .08 + 1.4(.10) = .22$

4. a. $E(r) = .05 + 0(.06) + 1(.08) = .13$
   b. $E(r) = .05 + 1(.06) + 0(.08) = .11$
   c. $E(r) = .05 + .5(.06) + .5(.08) = .12$
   d. $E(r) = .05 + 1(.06) + 1(.08) = .19$

5. a. $E(r) = .07 + .4(.08) + .4(.04) = .118$
   b. $E(r) = .07 + .4(.08) + 1.2(.04) = .15$
   c. $E(r) = .07 + .6(.08) + .8(.04) = .15$
   d. $E(r) = .07 + .9(.08) + 1.1(.04) = .186$

6. A. $E(r) = .04 + .8(.06) + .4(.04) + .6(.08) = .152$
   b. $E(r) = .04 + 1.2(.06) + .8(.04) + .2(.08) = .16$
   c. $E(r) = .04 + 1.3(.06) + .9(.04) + .3(.08) = .178$

7. a. $E(r) = .08 + 2(.10) + 1(.04) + 1(.06) = .38$
   b. $E(r) = .08 + .5(.10) + .5(.04) + .5(.06) = .18$
   c. $E(r) = .08 + 0(.10) + 1(.04) + .5(.06) = .15$

8. A earns .08 more than B and its beta is .8 larger. This implies the factor risk premium is .10. The risk-free rate then must be $.20 - 1.3(.10) = .07$.

9. A and C have the same $beta_2$, but C has a $beta_2$ that is .4 greater than that of A. The difference in returns is .024 which implies a factor one risk premium of .06. B and C have the same $beta_1$, but B has a $beta_2$ that is 1 greater. The .08 difference in their returns implies a factor two risk premium of .08. The risk-free rate therefore is $.104 - .4(.06) - .5(.08) = .04$.

10. Yes, an equally-weighted portfolio of A and B has a return of .05 in state 1, .08 in state 2, and .12 in state 3. The portfolio offers a higher return in every state than does stock C.

11.

	Dollar Investment	Payoff$_1$	Payoff$_2$	Payoff$_3$
portfolio	1,000,000	1,050,000	1,080,000	1,120,000
C	-1,000,000	-1,040,000	-1,060,000	-1,080,000
net	0	10,000	20,000	40,000

12. To eliminate the arbitrage possibility, the price of C must fall enough to raise its return above that of the portfolio in at least one of the states. The returns are closest in state 1, so solving

the expression 10.40/price = 1.05 we find that at a price of $9.90, asset C's return is greater than .05.

13. The returns to an equally weighted portfolio of D and F are .12 in state 1, .10 in state 2, and .10 in state 3.

14.

	Dollar Investment	Payoff$_1$	Payoff$_2$	Payoff$_3$
portfolio	10,000,000	11,200,000	11,000,000	11,000,000
E	-10,000,000	-11,000,000	-10,900,000	-10,800,000
net	0	200,000	100,000	200,000

15. Solving 21.80/price = 1.10, we find that at a price of $19.81, D's return exceeds .10.

16. C

17. .06 = 1 (.04) + .7 (-.12) + e
    e = .06 - .04 + (.084)
    e = .1040

11 Equilibrium with Multiple Sources of Risk: The Multifactor CAPM

OUTLINE

I. The multifactor CAPM

    A. Additional sources of risk

    B. Hedging demands

    C. The multifactor security market line (SML)

II. APT vs. the multifactor CAPM

HIGHLIGHTS

Investors face many risks in addition to market risk, which is the only risk considered in the standard CAPM. Examples of risks that investors may wish to hedge include uncertainty about the future relative prices of consumption goods, uncertainty about future labor income, and uncertainty about future investment opportunities. If a portfolio of securities exists that is correlated with an extra-market source of uncertainty, investors may use the portfolio to hedge against this risk. In this case the multifactor CAPM is applicable, and security returns involve additional risk premia based on the additional sources of risk. The multifactor CAPM is an identical pricing expression to the multifactor APT.

PROBLEMS

All the problems are related.

1. Consider an investor with an annual labor income of $50,000, which he consumes, and an investment portfolio of $200,000. The income from the portfolio is also consumed each year. The investment portfolio consists of T-bills that earn 8% and a market-index fund with an expected return of 16% and a standard deviation of 30%. If the investor places 40% of his wealth in the index fund, what are the expected value and standard deviation of his expenditure budget?

2. The investor is currently spending $25,000 on food items, and he will consume the same amount regardless of prices. Food prices are not expected to increase but are risky, and the standard deviation of the rate of increase is 20%. What is the expected value of the consumption budget (total expenditures less food expenditures)?

3. What is the standard deviation of the consumption budget?

4. What is the marginal risk to the investor from food-price uncertainty?

5. If the investor wishes to bring the risk of the consumption budget down to the level it was before food-price uncertainty was considered, what percentage of the portfolio should be invested in the index fund?

6. What is the expected value of the expenditure budget if the investor shifts funds from the index fund to T-bills?

7. What is the standard deviation of the expenditure budget?

8. What is the standard deviation of the consumption budget?

9. If there is a mutual fund that is perfectly correlated with food prices and uncorrelated with the market index, should the investor take a long or short position in the fund to hedge food-price uncertainty?

10. What is the expected return on the fund? It has a zero beta.

11. If the standard deviation of the food-related mutual fund is .25, how much money should be placed in the fund to eliminate food-price uncertainty?

12. What are the amounts placed in T-bills and the index fund?

13. What are the expected value and standard deviation of the consumption budget if the investor hedges with the food-related fund?

SOLUTIONS

1. $E(B) = 50{,}000 + 200{,}000\,[.08 + .4(.08)] = \$72{,}400$
   std dev $= 200{,}000\,(.4)(.3) = \$24{,}000$

2. $E(C) = 72{,}400 - 25{,}000 = \$47{,}400$

3. std dev $= [24{,}000^2 + 25{,}000^2\,(.2)^2]^{.5}$
   $= \$24{,}515.30$

4. marginal increment to risk $= 24{,}515 - 24{,}000 = \$515$

5. want consumption risk $= 24{,}000$
   std dev $= 24{,}000 = (x^2 + 5000^2)^{.5}$
   $576{,}000{,}000 - 25{,}000{,}000 = x^2$
   $x = \$23{,}473.39$

   To get the standard deviation of the expenditure budget to $23,473.39, invest 39.12% of the portfolio in the index fund.

6. $E(B) = 50{,}000 + 200{,}000\,[.08 + .3912\,(.08)] = \$72{,}259.20$

7. std dev $= 200{,}000\,(.3912)(.3) = \$23{,}473.39$

8. std dev $= (23{,}473.39^2 + 5000^2)^{.5}$
   $= \$24{,}000$

9. Take a long position: as food prices increase, the return on the fund will offset the increased expenditures.

10. If the fund has a zero beta and the simple CAPM holds, it will earn the T-bill rate, 8%.

11. $25{,}000\,(.2/.25) = \$20{,}000$

12. The $20,000 in the food fund will come from T-bills so that $100,000 will remain in T-bills and $80,000 in the market fund.

13. By hedging with the food-related fund, the expected consumption budget is $47,400 with a standard deviation of $24,000.

12 Empirical Evidence on Security Returns

OUTLINE

I. The index model and the single-factor APT

   A. Estimating beta

   B. Estimating the SML

   C. Results of tests

II. Roll's critique

   A. Unobservability of the market portfolio

   B. Efficiency of the proxy portfolio

   C. Results of mutual funds tests

III. Multifactor models

   A. Factor analysis

   B. Prespecified hedge portfolios

HIGHLIGHTS

Early tests of the single-factor CAPM, after controlling for measurement error, supported the zero-beta version of the CAPM; the slope was too flat and the intercept too high for the standard CAPM to hold. Richard Roll pointed out that the CAPM was untestable as the true market portfolio cannot be identified. As a result, a proxy for the market portfolio must be used. If the proxy chosen turns out to be efficient, ex post, then there is a linear relationship between beta and expected return. If the proxy is ex post inefficient, then the expected linear risk-return relationship is not observed. Thus, all that can be concluded from the type of test performed earlier is whether or not the proxy was efficient. The tests tell one nothing about the validity of the model. While the CAPM cannot be tested, the superiority of returns to market indices to those of professionally managed portfolios support the efficiency of those indices. Research indicates that more than one factor is important in security returns. Factor analysis yields insight as to the number of factors, but not as to what the factors are. To yield an implementable theory, continued work with prespecified factors is necessary.

PROBLEMS

1. Given the results below from a regression involving 31 observations, classify each coefficient as significantly different from zero at the 95% level or not.

Coefficient	Standard Error
$B_0 = .114$	.058
$B_1 = .047$	.009
$B_2 = .290$	.158
$B_3 = .012$	.003

2. For the following results of a regression involving 61 observations, determine the P-value for the test that the coefficient is zero.

Coefficient	Standard Error
$B_0 = .01016$	.04
$B_1 = .08148$	.12
$B_2 = .25065$	.15
$B_3 = .07776$	.06

SOLUTIONS

1. The T-test is a two tailed test, so the cut-off value is the .975 fractile. For 30 degrees of freedom (one less than the number of observations) the value is 2.042.

    $T_o = .114/.058 = 1.966$

    $T_1 = .047/.009 = 5.222$

    $T_2 = .290/.158 = 1.835$

    $T_3 = .012/.003 = 4$

    B_1, B_3 are significantly different from zero.

2. Calculating T-Values.

    $T_o = .01016/.04 = .254$

    $T_1 = .08148/.12 = .679$

    $T_2 = .25065/.15 = 1.671$

    $T_3 = .07776/.06 = 1.296$

Coefficient	T-Value	Fractile	P
B_0	.254	.6	.8
B_1	.679	.75	.5
B_2	1.671	.95	.10
B_3	1.296	.9	.20

13 Market Efficiency

OUTLINE

I. Stock prices as a random walk

II. The Efficient Markets Hypothesis (EMH)

    A. Weak form

    B. Semi-strong form

    C. Strong form

III. Implications of the EMH

    A. Technical analysis

    B. Fundamental analysis

    C. Active vs. passive portfolio management

IV. Tests of the EMH

    A. Weak-form tests

    B. Semi-strong-form tests

        1. Abnormal returns

        2. Joint test of efficiency and the assumed return generating process.

    C. Strong-form tests.

HIGHLIGHTS

The Efficient Markets Hypothesis states that current stock prices fully reflect all available information. The hypothesis has three forms, and each form refers to a different information set that is reflected in price. The weak form deals with all market information, and weak-form efficiency means that technical analysis is useless. The semi-strong form deals with public information, and semi-strong-form efficiency implies that fundamental analysis (if it uses only public information) will not yield abnormal returns. The strong form of the hypothesis is concerned with all information, public and private. If the market were strong-form efficient, no abnormal profits could be made by anyone, even with inside information. The empirical evidence strongly supports weak-form and semi-strong-form market efficiency and supports strong-form inefficiency. There are, however, instances in which the market does appear to be semi-strong inefficient, such as the small firm and January effects. Since, in testing for semi-strong efficiency, an assumption must be made, as to what a normal return would be these anomalies may be the result of an incorrectly specified return-generating process. One of the most important results of the efficient markets studies has been the growth of index funds. Market efficiency implies that a passive strategy of buying and holding a broad-based market index will yield a higher return than actively researching and managing a portfolio of specific stocks.

PROBLEMS

1. Given you believe the following model explains returns in excess of the risk-free rate for stock A, what are the expected returns in each year? The T-bill rate is 6%.

    $R_A = .01 + 1.2 R_M$

    a. market return = .12
    b. market return = .14
    c. market return = -.05
    d. market return = .03

2. Answer Problem 1 for stock B, whose returns in excess of the risk-free rate are given by

    $R_B = .03 + .5 R_M$

3. The following are monthly returns to stock C and the market, relative to the announcement of a stock split. Calculate the abnormal returns, given the model below for returns in excess of the risk-free rate. The monthly T-bill rate is 1%.

$$R_C = .02 + 1.5\, R_M$$

Month	Market Return	Stock Return
-4	.01	.05
-3	.02	.05
-2	-.01	.03
-1	.03	.08
0	.02	.045
1	.01	.04

4. For the stock in Problem 3, calculate the cumulative abnormal returns (CARs).

5. Do the results suggest the market is efficient with respect to stock splits?

6. The following are daily returns to stock D and the market, relative to an information announcement. Calculate the abnormal returns, given the model below.

$$R_D = .003 + .8\, R_M$$

Day	Market Return	Stock Return
-5	.005	0
-4	.001	.004
-3	.003	.006
-2	-.002	.002
-1	-.001	.002
0	.010	.015
1	.005	.009
2	-.009	.001

7. For the stock in Problem 6, calculate the cumulative abnormal returns.

8. Do the results suggest leakage of information?

9. Do the results suggest that an abnormal profit could be made by purchasing the stock after the announcement?

CFA PROBLEM

10. (CFA Examination 1987, Level I) An "efficient market" is one in which:

    a. the commissions on large transactions are smaller than the commissions on small transactions
    b. new information is quickly reflected in the prices of securities
    c. little time and effort are spent on marketing securities to the general public
    d. the cost of receiving, processing, executing, and reporting completed orders is very small

SOLUTIONS

1. a. $E(r) = .06 + .01 + 1.2(.12) = .214$
   b. $E(r) = .06 + .01 + 1.2(.14) = .238$
   c. $E(r) = .06 + .01 + 1.2(-.05) = .01$
   d. $E(r) = .06 + .01 + 1.2(.03) = .106$

2. a. $E(r) = .06 + .03 + .5(.12) = .15$
   b. $E(r) = .06 + .03 + .5(.14) = .16$
   c. $E(r) = .06 + .03 + .5(-.05) = .065$
   d. $E(r) = .06 + .03 + .5(.03) = .105$

3.
Month	E(r)		Abnormal Return
-4	$.01 + .02 + 1.5(.01)$	$= .045$	$.05 - .045 = .005$
-3	$.01 + .02 + 1.5(.02)$	$= .06$	$.05 - .06 = -.01$
-2	$.01 + .02 + 1.5(-.01)$	$= .015$	$.03 - .015 = .015$
-1	$.01 + .02 + 1.5(.03)$	$= .075$	$.08 - .075 = .005$
0	$.01 + .02 + 1.5(.02)$	$= .06$	$.045 - .06 = .015$
1	$.01 + .02 + 1.5(.01)$	$= .045$	$.04 - .045 = -.005$

4.
Month	CAR			
-4	.005			
-3	.005	- .01	=	-.005
-2	-.005	+ .015	=	.01
-1	.01	+ .005	=	.015
0	.015	- .015	=	0
1	0 +	- .005	=	-.005

5. Yes, the CARs are very close to zero, indicating that the information contained in the stock split announcement is already impounded in stock price four months before the split.

6. As daily returns are used, the risk-free yield can be ignored as it is negligible on a daily basis.

Day	Expected Return			Abnormal Return		
-5	.003 + .8(-.005)	=	-.001	0 - (-.001)	=	.001
-4	.003 + .8(.001)	=	.0038	.004 - .0038	=	.0002
-3	.003 + .8(.003)	=	.0054	.006 - .0054	=	.0006
-2	.003 + .8(-.002)	=	.0014	.002 - .0014	=	.0006
-1	.003 + .8(-.001)	=	.0022	.002 - .0022	=	-.0002
0	.003 + .8(.010)	=	.011	.015 - .011	=	.004
1	.003 + .8(.005)	=	.007	.009 - .007	=	.002
2	.003 + .8(-.009)	=	-.0042	.001 - (-.0042)	=	.0052

4.
Day	CAR			
-5	.001			
-4	.001	+ .0002	=	.0012
-3	.0012	+ .006	=	.0018
-2	.0018	+ .0006	=	.0024
-1	.0024	+ -.002	=	.0022
0	.0022	+ .004	=	.0062
1	.0062	+ .002	=	.0082
2	.0082	+ .0052	=	.0134

8. Yes, to the degree that the CARs are consistently rising prior to the announcement.

9. Yes; while there is a large adjustment on the day of the announcement, there is continued abnormal performance on days 1 and 2.

10. b

14 Bond Prices and Yields

OUTLINE

I. Bond pricing

    A. Price is the present value of expected cash flows

    B. Yield to maturity

    C. Bond prices over time

II. Treasury securities

    A. Zero - coupon bonds

    B. Coupon bonds

III. Corporate bonds

    A. Bond ratings

    B. Bond indentures

    C. Callable bonds

    D. Convertible bonds

    E. Floating-rate bonds

HIGHLIGHTS

A bond is an IOU issued by a corporation or government. A typical coupon bond obligates the issuer to make specified interest payments at specific times and to repay the principal or face value at maturity. A zero-coupon bond pays no interest, and the investor's return is in the form of capital gains. Treasury securities are risk-free as there is no possibility of default, while corporate bonds are rated by firms such as Moody's and Standard and Poor's according to the estimated probability of default. The market price of a bond is the present value of the cash flow to be received from it, where the discount rate is the yield to maturity. The yield to maturity is the rate of return that the investor would earn if the bond were held to maturity and the coupon payments invested at that same rate. The prices of bonds fluctuate with interest rates, rising as interest rates decline. The bond indenture is a contract between the issuer and bondholders that includes restrictions on the actions the firm may take, in order to protect bondholders. Callable bonds give the company the right to retire the bond before the maturity date, while put bonds allow the bondholder to extend the maturity of the bond. Convertible bonds allow the bondholder to exchange the bond for a specified number of shares of common stock, allowing the investor to share in the good fortunes of the company while affording him the fixed income associated with a bond.

PROBLEMS

1. What is the price of a $1000 face value bond with five years to maturity, if the coupon rate is 8% and interest payments are made annually? The yield to maturity is 10%.

2. Answer Problem 1 assuming semiannual coupon payments.

3. What is the price of a $1000 face value bond with six years to maturity, a 12% coupon rate, and semiannual coupon payments if the yield to maturity is 10%?

4. Answer Problem 3 assuming the yield to maturity is 12%.

5. Consider a $1000 face value bond with one year to maturity. If the coupon rate is 10% and interest payments are made annually, calculate the change in the price of the bond if the yield to maturity changes from 10% to 12%. What is the change in price if the yield to maturity changes from 10% to 8%?

6. Answer Problem 5 assuming the bond has five years to maturity.

7. Answer Problem 5 assuming the bond has ten years to maturity.

8. Calculate the effective annual yield to maturity for the following bonds that pay interest semiannually:
   a. YTM = .10
   b. YTM = .16
   c. YTM = .18

9. What is the yield to maturity for a $1000 face value, 8% coupon, three-year bond with annual interest payments if the current price is $950.26?

10. What is the yield to maturity for a $1000 face value, 12% coupon, five-year bond with annual interest payments if the current price is $1036.96?

11. What is the yield to maturity for a two-year, $1000 face value bond with a 10% coupon if the price is $964.35 and coupon payments are made semiannually?

12. What is the yield to maturity for the bond in Problem 11 if the price is $1036.29?

13. Calculate the effective yield on the following T-bills:
    a. 1 month selling at $99,000
    b. 2 month selling at $98,500
    c. 3 month selling at $96,000

14. A $1000 face value bond is convertible into 25 shares of stock and is currently selling for $900. If the stock is currently selling for $30, what is the conversion premium?

15. The current stock price is $40 and a $1000 face value bond is selling for $1400. If there is a $200 conversion premium, for how many shares may the convertible be exchanged?

CFA PROBLEMS

16. (CFA Examination 1985, Level I) What is the current yield of a $10,000 bond bearing a 14% coupon rate and having a current market price of 95?

    a. 14.00%
    b. 14.74%
    c. 15.36%
    d. Insufficient information provided.

17. (CFA Examination 1987, Level I) When computing yield-to-maturity, the implicit reinvestment assumption is that the interest payments will be reinvested at the:

    a. coupon rate
    b. prime rate
    c. computed yield-to-maturity rate.
    d. market rates prevailing when the payments are made

18. (CFA Examination 1985, Level I) When can a bond with a "deferred call" be retired?

    a. At any time prior to maturity if the issuer gives reasonable notice
    b. After a specified period following the date of issue
    c. At any time, but the issuer will have to pay all accrued interest
    d. Before its maturity date by issuing a similar term bond carrying a higher promised yield

19. (CFA Examination 1985, Level I) Suppose the marginal income tax rate is 25% and a tax-free municipal bond is purchased with a yield of 11%. This yield would be equivalent to that received on a taxable bond with a yield of:

    a. 12.15%
    b. 13.53%
    c. 14.67%
    d. 15.53%

20. (CFA Examination 1985, Level I) It is true that bonds issued by all agencies of the United States government:

    a. are exempt from federal income tax
    b. become direct obligations of the United States Treasury
    c. are secured bonds backed by government holdings
    d. none of the above

21. (CFA Examination 1985, Level I) McLaughlin Corporation sold an 8%, $1,000,000 bond issue at a price to yield 9%. The bond pays

interest semiannually. How much cash would be paid by McLaughlin at each interest payment date?

a. $40,000
b. $45,000
c. $80,000
d. $90,000

SOLUTIONS

1. P = PV(coupon pmts) + PV(1000)
    = 80 (PVIFA 10%, 5) + 1000(PVIF 10%, 5)
    = 303.26 + 620.92
    = 924.18

2. P = 40(PVIFA .5%, 10) + 1000(PVIF 5%, 10)

    = 308.87 + 613.91
    = 922.78

3. P = 60(PVIFA 5%, 12) + 1000(PVIF 5%, 12)
    = 531.80 + 556.84
    = 1088.64

4. When the coupon rate is equal to the yield to maturity, the bond sells for its face value. In Problems 1 and 2 the yield to maturity is greater than the coupon rate, so the bond sells at a discount. In Problem 3 the yield to maturity is less than the coupon rate, so the bond sells at a premium.

5. The price of the bond at a 10% YTM is $1000.
    YTM = 12%, P = 1100/1.12 = $982.14
    YTM = 8%, P = 1100/1.08 = $1018.52
    If the YTM changes from 10% to 12%, the percentage change is (982.14 -1000)/1000 = -1.786%.
    If the YTM changes from 10% to 8% the percentage change is (1018.52 -1000)/1000 = 1.852%

6. YTM = 10%, P = $1000
    YTM = 12%, P = 100(PVIFA 12%, 5) + 1000(PVIF 12%, 5) = $927.91
    YTM = 8%, P = 100(PVIFA 8%, 5) + 1000(PVIF 12%, 5) = $1079.85
    10% - 12%, percentage change = (927.91 -1000)/1000 = -7.209%
    10% - 8%, percentage change = (1079.85 - 1000)/1000 = 7.985%

7. YTM = 10%, P = $1000
    YTM = 12%, P = 100(PVIFA 12%, 10) + 1000(PVIF 12%, 10) = $886.99
    YTM = 8%, P = 100(PVIFA 8%, 10) + 1000(PVIF 8%, 10) = $1134.20
    10% - 12%, percentage change = (886.99 -1000)/1000 = -11.30%
    10% - 8%, percentage change = (1134.20 -1000)/1000 = 13.42%

8. a. $(1.05)^2 - 1 = .1025$
    b. $(1.08)^2 - 1 = .1664$
    c. $(1.09)^2 - 1 = .1881$

9. 10%

10. 11%

11. 12%

12. 8%

13. a. The one-month yield = 1000/99000 = .0101
       annual yield = $(1.0101)^{12} - 1 = .1282$

    b. two-month yield = 1500/98500 = .01523
       annual yield = $(1.01523)^6 - 1 = .0949$

    c. three-month yield = 4000/96000 = .04167
       annual yield = $(1.04167)^4 - 1 = .1774$

14. conversion value = 30 x 25 = $750
    conversion premium = 900 - 750 = $150

15. conversion value = 1400 - 200 = $1200
    1200/40 = 30 shares

16. b

17. c

18. b

19. c

20. d

21. a

15 The Term Structure of Interest Rates

OUTLINE

I. The term structure under certainty

    A. The long-term rate is the average of the short-term rates

    B. Holding period return

    C. Forward rates equal future short rates

II. Measuring the yield curve

III. Interest rate uncertainty

IV. Theories of the term structure

    A. Expectations hypothesis

    B. Liquidity preference

    C. Market segmentation and preferred habitat

V. Interpreting the yield curve

VI. Realized compound yield to maturity

HIGHLIGHTS

The term structure of interest rates is the relationship between interest rate and maturity for securities that differ only in time to maturity. The graphical representation of this relationship is the yield curve. A yield curve constructed using only zero-coupon bonds is referred to as the pure yield curve. Under certainty, the long rates are the average of the current and future short rates. Under uncertainty, the future short rates are unknown, and the short rates inferred from the long rates are known as forward rates. Four theories have been proposed to explain the shape of the yield curve. The expectations theory states that long rates are the geometric average of the current and expected short rates. The liquidity preference theory states that short-term investors dominate the market, so that long rates are higher than short rates. Market segmentation states that investors do not consider all maturities and the short rates are set independently of the long rates. Preferred habitat follows this line of reasoning, but states that investors will move between markets if the premiums are sufficient. The realized compound yield to maturity is an alternative to the conventional yield to maturity and is superior if future short rates are known, but has no clear advantage under interest rate uncertainty.

PROBLEMS

1. Assume the following short rates are known with certainty. Calculate the long rates.

Year	Rate
0	.07
1	.09
2	.10
3	.11

2. Assume the following short rates are known with certainty. Calculate the long rates.

Year	Rate
0	.14
1	.12
2	.10
3	.08

3. Assume the following rates are known with certainty. Calculate the future short rates.

Maturity	Rate
1	.08
2	.09
3	.10
4	.12

4. Assume the following rates are known with certainty. Calculate the future short rates.

Maturity	Rate
1	.14
2	.12
3	.11
4	.09

5. Given the following prices of zero-coupon bonds, calculate the yield to maturity of each bond and the implied forward rates.

Maturity	Price
1	$925.93
2	$841.58
3	$751.31
4	$658.73

6. Given the following prices of zero-coupon bonds, calculate the yield to maturity and the implied forward rates.

Maturity	Price
1	$909.09
2	$841.68
3	$793.83
4	$762.90

7. What is the realized compound yield of each of the bonds in Problem 6?

8. Consider a 10% coupon, $1000 face bond with three years to maturity making annual coupon payments. The following interest rates will hold in the next three years with certainty: $r_1 = .10$, $r_2 = .12$, $r_3 = .14$. What is the price of the bond and the yield to maturity?

9. What is the realized compound yield of the bond in Problem 8?

10. Consider a 12% coupon, $1000 face bond with four years to maturity making annual interest payments. The following interest rates are known with certainty: $r_1 = .12$, $r_2 = .10$, $r_3 = .08$, $r_4 = .06$. What is the yield to maturity of the bond?

11. What is the realized compound yield of the bond in Problem 10?

12. The following are yields on zero-coupon bonds. Assume the expectations hypothesis of the term structure holds. Calculate the yield curve that is expected to hold in one year.

Maturity	Yield
1	.09
2	.11
3	.12

13. Using the information in Problem 12, what is the current price of a three-year, $1000 face, 10% coupon bond making annual interest payments? What is the price expected to be in one year?

14. Using the information in Problem 12, what is expected rate of return from holding the bond one year?

15. Using the information in Problem 12, suppose the yield curve flattens out at .10 after one year. What is the return from holding the bond one year?

16. Using the information in Problem 12, suppose the yield curve flattens out at .14 after one year. What is the return from holding the bond one year?

CFA PROBLEMS

17. (CFA Examination 1985, Level I) In explaining the shape of yield curves, the expectation hypothesis asserts that:

    a. once a flat yield curve has been established, it will stabilize
    b. the yield curve is primarily explained by the interest rate anticipations of investors
    c. yield curves take an ascending form due to the compounding effect
    d. descending yield curves are typical

18. (CFA Examination, 1985, Level I) Which theory explains the shape of the yield curve by considering the relative demands for various maturities?

    a. Unbiased expectations theory
    b. Liquidity preference theory
    c. Segmentation theory
    d. Relative strength theory

19. (CFA Examination 1985, Level I) A portfolio manager who subscribed to the liquidity preference hypothesis would expect:

    a. that longer-term securities will tend to promise higher returns
    b. rational investors to pay a price premium for a shorter-term security
    c. long-term rates to be higher than expected, due to the existence of a liquidity premium
    d. all of the above

20. (CFA Examination 1985, Level I) A yield curve depicts the relationship between yield and:

    a. safety
    b. maturity date
    c. risk
    d. coupon rate

21. (CFA Examination 1982, Level I)

    a. Explain what is meant by the term structure of interest rates. Explain the theoretical basis of an upward-sloping yield curve.

    b. Explain the economic circumstances under which you would expect to see the inverted yield curve prevail.

SOLUTIONS

1. 2 yr. rate = $[(1.07)(1.09)]^{.5} - 1 = .07995$

   3 yr. rate = $[(1.07)(1.09)(1.10)]^{.33} - 1 = .08659$

   4 yr. rate = $[(1.07)(1.09)(1.10)(1.11)]^{.25} - 1 = .0934$

2. 2 yr. rate = $[(1.14)(1.12)]^{.5} - 1 = .12996$

   3 yr. rate = $[(1.14)(1.12)(1.10)]^{.33} - 1 = .11988$

   4 yr. rate = $[(1.14)(1.12)(1.10)(1.08)]^{.25} - 1 = .10977$.

3. $r_1 = .08$

   $r_2 = 1.09^2/1.08 - 1 = .10009$

   $r_3 = 1.10^3/1.09^2 - 1 = .12028$

   $r_4 = 1.12^4/1.10^3 - 1 = .18221$

4. $r_1 = .14$

   $r_2 = 1.12^2/1.14 - 1 = .10035$

   $r_3 = 1.11^3/1.12^2 - 1 = .09027$

   $r_4 = 1.09^4/1.11^3 - 1 = .03214$

5. 1 yr $1000/925.93 = 1 + k$ $k = .08$

   2 yr $\frac{1000}{841.68} = (1 + k)^2$ $k = .09$

   3 yr $\frac{1000}{751.31} = (1 + k)^3$ $k = .10$

   4 yr $\frac{1000}{658.73} = (1 + k)^4$ $k = .11$

   $f_2 = (1.09)^2/1.08 - 1 = .10009$

   $f_3 = (1.10)^3/(1.09)^2 - 1 = .12028$

   $f_4 = (1.11)^4/(1.10)^3 - 1 = .14055$

6. 1 yr $\frac{1000}{909.09} = 1 + k \quad k = .10$

    2 yr $\frac{1000}{841.68} = (1 + k)^2 \quad k = .09$

    3 yr $\frac{1000}{793.83} = (1 + k)^3 \quad k = .08$

    4 yr $\frac{1000}{762.90} = (1 + k)^4 \quad k = .07$

    $f_2 = (1.09)^2/1.10 - 1 = .08009$

    $f_3 = (1.08)^3/(1.09)^2 - 1 = .06027$

    $f_4 = (1.07)^4/(1.08)^3 - 1 = .04055$

7. As the bonds are zero coupon, the realized compound yield is the same as the yield to maturity.

8.
Time	Cash Flow	Discount Factor	Present Value
1	100	1.10	90.91
2	100	(1.10)(1.12)	81.17
3	1100	(1.10)(1.12)(1.14)	783.21
			$955.29

    The price of the bond is $955.29.
    The yield to maturity is the single interest rate that equates the present value of the cash flows with the price; in this case it is .1185.

9. Value of cash flows at time 3

    $100(1.12)(1.14) = 127.68$
    $100(1.14) = 114$
    $ 1100$
    $ \overline{1341.68}$

    $955.29 (1 + y)^3 = 1341.68 \quad y = .11988$

10.
Time	Cash Flows	Discount Factor	Present Value
1	120	1.12	107.14
2	120	(1.12)(1.10)	97.40
3	120	(1.12)(1.10)(1.08)	90.19
4.	1120	(1.12)(1.10)(1.08)(1.06)	794.10
			$1088.83

    Finding the single rate that equates price and the present value of the cash flow, the yield to maturity is .0925.

11. Value of cash flows at time 4

    $$120(1.10)(1.08)(1.06) = 151.11$$
    $$120(1.08)(1.06) = 137.38$$
    $$120(1.06) = 127.20$$
    $$1120$$
    $$\$1535.69$$

    $1088.83 (1 + y)^4 = 1535.69 \quad y = .08977$

12. Currently $f_2 = 1.11^2/1.09 - 1 = .13037$

    $f_3 = 1.12^3/1.11^2 - 1 = .14027$

    in one year
    1 yr rate = .13037
    2 yr rate = $[(1.13037)(1.14027)]^{.5} - 1 = .13531$

13. currently

Time	Cash Flow	Discount Factor	Present Value
1	100	1.09	91.74
2	100	(1.09)(1.13037)	81.16
3	1100	(1.09)(1.13037)(1.14027)	782.96
			$955.86

    in one year

Time	Cash Flow	Discount Factor	Present Value
1	100	1.13037	88.47
2	1100	(1.13037)(1.14027)	853.42
			$941.89

14. $\dfrac{(941.89 - 955.86 + 100)}{955.96} = .09$

15. price = $100/1.10 + 1100/1.10^2 = \$1000$

    return = $\dfrac{(1000 - 955.86 + 100)}{955.86} = .1508$

16. price = $100/1.14 + 1100/1.14^2 = 934.13$

    return = $\dfrac{(934.13 - 955.86 + 100)}{955.86} = .0819$

17. b

18. c

19. d

20. b

21. a. The term structure of interest rates refers to the relationship between yields and maturities for fixed-income securities of the same or similar issuer. Expectations regarding future interest rate levels give rise to differing supply and demand pressures in the various maturity sectors of the bond market. These pressures are reflected in differences in the yield movements of bonds of different maturity.

    The "term structure of interest rates," or "yield curve," will normally be upward sloping in a period of relatively stable price expectations. The theoretical basis for the upward sloping yield curve is the fact that investors generally demand a premium, the longer the maturity of the issue, to cover risk through time.

    b. According to the expectations theory of yield curve determination, if borrowers prefer to sell short-maturity issues at the time lenders prefer to invest in longs, as is the case when interest rates are expected to fall, longer-maturity issues will tend to yield less than shorter-maturity issues. The yield curve will be downward sloping. This generally occurs in periods such as the past several years when restrictive monetary policy by the Federal Reserve System, in an attempt to control inflation and inflation expectations, resulted in very high short-term interest rates. In these circumstances, demand for longer-term maturities is severely dampened.

16 Fixed Income Portfolio Management

OUTLINE

I. Interest rate risk

    A. Price risk

    B. Reinvestment rate risk

II. Duration

III. Passive bond management

    A. Net worth immunization

    B. Target date immunization

    C. Cash flow matching and dedication

IV. Active bond management

    A. Bond swaps

    B. Horizon analysis

    C. Contingent immunization

    D. Interest rate swaps

HIGHLIGHTS

All bonds are subject to interest rate risk. As interest rates change, the price of the bond and the rate at which coupons are reinvested also change. These risks are in opposite directions: as the interest rate rises, the price of the bond falls, but the reinvestment rate rises. As the interest rate falls, the price of the bond rises, but the reinvestment rate falls. The point in time where the two risks exactly offset is given by the duration of the bond. Duration is a measure of the average life of a bond and also a measure of the sensitivity of bond price to changes in the interest rate. Management of bond portfolios can be classified as active or passive. The passive strategies attempt to render the portfolio immune from changes in interest rates. The immunization strategies focus on preserving net worth, matching cash flows, or locking in the future value of the portfolio. To lock in the future value of the portfolio, the manager chooses a portfolio whose duration is equal to the planned holding period. The portfolio must be rebalanced as time passes and interest rates change. Active management consists of choosing securities based on interest rate forecasts and the analysis of yield differentials between securities. Interest rate swaps consist of trading the cash flows on securities while holding on to the securities, and provide a low-cost way of managing interest rate risk.

PROBLEMS

1. Calculate the prices of a one-year, three-year, and five-year 10% coupon bond at a 10% yield to maturity (YTM). What are the changes in price if the YTM falls to 9%? The coupons are paid annually.

2. Calculate the duration of each of the bonds in Problem 1 at a 10% YTM.

3. Use the approximation and duration figures from Problem 2 to calculate the approximate change in price for each of the bonds in Problem 1.

4. What is the duration of a perpetuity that pays $250 once a year forever at a yield of 9%? What is the duration at 7%?

5. Calculate the duration of a seven-year annual annuity with $200 payments if the yield is 10%.

6. Answer Problem 5 if the yield is 8%.

7. Answer Problem 5 if the yield is 12%.

8. Calculate the duration of a 10% coupon bond with annual coupons and a six-year maturity if the YTM = 10%.

9. Answer Problem 8 if the coupons are paid semiannually.

10. What is the duration of a 14% coupon bond with five years to maturity if the YTM = 10%? The coupons are paid annually.

11. Answer Problem 10 assuming coupons are paid semiannually.

12. What is the approximate change in price for the bond in Problem 10 if the YTM rises to 12%?

13. You have to have $29,386.56 in five years. The current YTM = 8% and you choose to immunize your portfolio by using $20,000 worth of six-year, 8% annual coupon bonds. Determine the end value of your portfolio under the following scenarios:
    a. YTM stays at 8%.
    b. YTM falls to 6%.
    c. YTM rises to 10%.

14. You wish to immunize your portfolio and lock in the value in eight years. You will use four-year zero coupon bonds and perpetuities. If the current interest rate is 10%, what are the weights of each asset in the portfolio?

15. If the interest rate stays at 10%, what will be the weights of the portfolio in Problem 14 in one year?

16. Answer Problem 15 assuming the interest rate rises to 12%.

CFA PROBLEMS

17. (CFA Examination 1985, Level I) Rank the following bonds in order of descending duration. Explain your reasoning. (No calculations required.)

    A: 15% coupon, 20-year, yield to maturity at 10%

    B: 15% coupon, 15-year, yield to maturity at 10%

    C: Zero-coupon, 20-year, yield to maturity at 10%

    D: 8% coupon, 20-year, yield to maturity at 10%

    E: 15% coupon, 15-year, yield to maturity at 15%

18. (CFA Examination 1984, Level I) Assume a $10,000 par value zero coupon bond with a term to maturity at issue of 10 years and a market yield of 8%.

    a. Determine the duration of the bond.

    b. Calculate the initial issue price of the bond at a market yield of 8%, assuming semiannual compounding.

    c. Twelve months after issue, this bond is selling to yield 12%. Calculate its then-current market price. Calculate your pretax rate of return assuming you owned this bond during the 12-month period.

19. (CFA Examination 1987, Level I) The price volatility of a variable rate note may be reduced by:

    a. eliminating any put features
    b. resetting the coupon rate frequently
    c. reducing the size of the issue
    d. downgrading the quality rating

20. (CFA Examination 1987, level I) The interest rate risk of a bond normally is:

   a. greater for shorter maturities
   b. lower for longer duration
   c. lower for higher coupons
   d. all of the above

21. (CFA Examination 1986, Level I) Interest rate risk means:

   a. a rise in interest rates will cause a loss of principal value for bondholder.
   b. a rise in interest rates will cause a gain of principal value for bondholder.
   c. a decline in interest rates will cause a loss of principal value for the bondholder.
   d. a decline in interest rates will not affect the principal value of the bond.

SOLUTIONS

1. At 10% all the bonds sell for $1000, the face value. At 9% the prices are:

   $P_1 = 1100/1.09 = \$1009.17$

   $P_3 = 100/1.09 + 100/1.09^2 + 1100/1.09^3 = \$1025.31$

   $P_5 = 100/1.09 + 100/1.09^2 + 100/1.09^3 + 100/1.09^4 + 1100/1.09^5$
   $= \$1038.90$

   The one-year bond increases in price by .92%, the three-year bond by 2.53%, and the five-year bond by 3.89%.

2. $D_1 = (1)\ PV(1100)/1000 = 1\ yr.$

   $D_3 = (1)\ PV(100)/1000 + (2)\ PV(100)/1000 + (3)\ PV(1100)/1000$
   $= .0909 + .1653 + 2.4793$

   $= 2.7355\ yrs.$

   $D_5 = (1)\ PV(100)/1000 + (2)\ PV(100)/1000 + (3)\ PV(100)/1000 + (4)\ PV(100)/1000 + (5)\ PV(1100)/1000$

   $= .0909 + .1653 + .2254 + .2732 + 3.4151$

   $= 4.1699\ yrs.$

3. One-year: $-1(-.01/1.10) = .91\%$
   Three-year: $-2.7355(-.01/1.10) = 2.49\%$

Five-year: $-4.1699(-.01/1.10) = 3.79\%$

4. $D_9 = 1.09/.09 = 12.1111$ yrs.

   $D_8 = 1.07/.07 = 15.2857$ yrs.

5. Using Rule 6

   $D = 1.10/.10 - 7/(1.10^7 - 1) = 3.6216$ yrs.

6. $D = 1.08/.08 - 7/1.08^7 - 1) = 3.6937$ yrs.

7. $D = 1.12/.12 - 7/(1.12^7 - 1) = 3.5515$ yrs.

8. Using Rule 7

   $D = 1.10/.10 - 1.10/[.10(1.10^6 - 1) + .10] = 4.7908$ yrs.

9. Using Rule 7

   $D = 1.05/.05 - 1.05/[.05(1.05^{12} - 1) + .05] = 9.3064$ half-years

   $= 4.6532$ yrs.

10. $D = 1.10/.10 - [1.10 + 5(.04)]/[.14(1.10^5 - 1) + .10] = 3.9908$ yrs.

11. $D = 1.05/.05 - [1.05 + 10(.02)]/[.07(1.05^{10} - 1) + .05] = 7.7053$ half-years

    $= 3.8527$ yrs.

12. $-3.9908\ (.02/1.10) = -7.256\%$

13. a. FV = $1600\ (1.08)^4 + 1600\ (1.08)^3 + 1600\ (1.08)^2$
        $+ 1600(1.08) + 1600 +$ proceeds from bond sale

        $= 2176.78 + 2015.54 + 1866.24 + 1728 + 1600 + 20{,}000$

        $= \$29{,}386.56$

    b. FV = $1600(1.06)^4 + 1600(1.06)^3 + 1600(1.06)^2 + 1600(1.06)$
        $+ 1600 +$ proceeds from bond sale

        $= 2019.96 + 1905.63 + 1797.76 + 1696 + 1600 + 20{,}377.36$

        $= \$29{,}396.71$

    c. FV = $1600(1.1)^4 + 1600(1.1)^3 + 1600(1.1)^2 + 1600\ (1.1)$
        $+ 1600 +$ proceeds from bond sale

        $= 2342.56 + 2129.60 + 1936 + 1760 + 1600 + 19{,}636.36$

    = $29,404.52

Note: The immunization here is less perfect than in Table 16.5. This is due to the larger changes in interest rates.

14. The duration of the zero coupon bonds is 4 years. The duration of the perpetuities is 11 years.
    w = weight in perpetuities

    $$11w + 4(1 - w) = 8$$
    $$7w = 4$$
    $$w = .5714$$

15. $11w + 3(1 - w) = 7$ one year less remaining
    $$8w = 4$$
    $$w = .5$$

16. The duration of the perpetuities is 9.3333 years.
    $$9.3333w + 3(1 - w) = 7$$
    $$6.3333w = 4$$
    $$w = .6316$$

17. In descending order: C, D, A, B, E

    Duration is positively related to maturity, but inversely related to coupon and yield to maturity. It is clear that the 20-year duration of the zero coupon bond C is the longest. At the same maturity and market yield are D and A, and since D has the lower coupon it has the longer duration. Bond B has the same coupon and market as A but shorter maturity and thus shorter duration. Finally, E has the same coupon and maturity as B but has a shorter duration because of its higher yield to maturity.

    The simplest (but not the most obvious) way to see this is to rank the conditions in terms of decreasing duration, in turn:

Coupon	Maturity	Market Yield	Bond
0	20	10	C
8	20	10	D
15	20	10	A
15	15	10	B
15	15	15	E

18. a. At 8% the bond has a 10-year duration. Obviously, the duration of a zero coupon bond is always equal to the term to maturity irrespective of the market rate.

    b. Present value factor at 4% for 20 periods is .456; therefore issue price is $4,560.

    c.   Present value factor at 6% for 18 periods is .350; therefore market value a year later is $3500. Therefore, the rate of return is:

$$\frac{3500 - 4560}{4560} = \frac{-1060}{4560} = -23.25\%$$

19. b

20. c

21. a

17 Equity Valuation

OUTLINE

I. Balance sheet valuation methods

   A. Book value

   B. Liquidation value

   C. Replacement value

II. Intrinsic value vs. market price

III. Discounted dividend models

   A. Constant growth models

      1. Convergence of price to intrinsic value
      2. Value and investment opportunities
      3. P/E ratios and investment opportunities

   B. Multi-stage growth models

      1. Two-stage model
      2. More-than-two-stage models
      3. H Model

IV. Capitalized earnings models

V. Free cash flow approach

VI. Inflation and equity valuation

VII. Behavior of the aggregate market

   A. Explaining past behavior

   B. Predicting future behavior

VIII. Contingent claims approach

HIGHLIGHTS

This chapter discusses methods by which a fundamental analyst determines the intrinsic value of a stock. The intrinsic value is the analyst's best guess as to what the stock should sell for. Some methods are based on balance sheet information and consider the intrinsic value to be the book value, the liquidation value, or the replacement value of assets less liabilities on a per share basis. Other methods determine the intrinsic value as the present value of expected earnings, free cash flow, or dividends. The simplest discounted dividend model assumes a constant growth rate in dividends, but any dividend pattern may be analyzed by the discounted dividend models. Other methods of estimating intrinsic value include the contingent claims approach and the often employed P/E ratio approach. In this approach, the empirically determined P/E ratio is multiplied by next year's estimated earnings to determine the intrinsic value of the stock. The level of stock prices is shown to be determined in large part by corporate profits and interest rates. The real rate of return on stocks is shown to be inversely related to inflation.

PROBLEMS

1. Given the following information, calculate the book value per share of the firm.

   ABC Balance Sheet

Assets	Claims on Assets
$500,000,000	Liabilities $300,000,000
	Common equity $200,000,000
	8,000,000 shares outstanding

2. If the assets can be liquidated at 80 cents on the dollar, calculate the liquidation value per share for the firm in Problem 1.

3. Calculate Tobin's q for the firm in Problem 1 assuming the assets can be replaced for 20% more than book value and the market price of the stock is $40/share.

4. You expect the price of DEF stock to be $42.50/share in one year and expect it to pay a dividend of $1.30 in one year. The current price of DEF is $38.75.

   a. What is the expected dividend yield, rate of price appreciation, and HPR of DEF?

   b. If DEF's beta is .9, the risk-free rate is 6%, and the expected rate of return on the market is 12%, what is the required rate of return on DEF?

   c. What is the intrinsic value of DEF stock? What does this indicate as to the percentage of DEF you should include in your portfolio?

5. Given the following information, decide whether each stock should be included in your portfolio in greater or lesser amounts than a passive strategy would dictate. The risk-free rate is 7%, and the expected return on the market is 17%.

Stock	$E(D_1)$	$E(P_1)$	Beta	Market Price
A	$2.00	$54.50	.8	$52
B	$1.15	$41.00	1.2	$33
C	$2.50	$22.50	1.4	$18
D	$1.40	$47.25	1.5	$43

6. GHI stock just paid a dividend of $3 and dividends are expected to grow at 6% annually forever. Calculate the intrinsic value of GMI stock given the following market capitalization rates:
   a. .13
   b. .15
   c. .17

7. JKL stock just paid a dividend of $2 and the required rate of return on JKL is .12. Calculate the intrinsic value of JKL stock given the following growth rates:
   a. .04
   b. .08
   c. .10

8. MNO stock just paid a dividend of $2.50. The dividends are expected to grow at 6% forever. The market capitalization rate is 15%.
   a. What is the intrinsic value of MNO?
   b. If the current market price is $25 and it is never expected to converge to the intrinsic value, what is the one-year HPR?
   c. If the current market price is $25 and it is expected to converge to the intrinsic value in one year, what is the one-year HPR?

9. PQR stock just paid a dividend of $3.20, and dividends are expected to grow at 5% forever. The required rate of return is 14%.
   a. Calculate the intrinsic value of PQR.
   b. Calculate the one-year HPR if the current market price is $35 and it is never expected to converge to the intrinsic value.
   c. Calculate the one-year HPR if price is expected to converge to the intrinsic value in one year.

10. Calculate the expected growth in earnings for the following stocks:

Stock	Dividend Payout	Expected ROE
A	.5	.10
B	.4	.10
C	.4	.15
D	.2	.15

11. Calculate the intrinsic value of each of the stocks in Problem 10 assuming each has a market capitalization rate of 14% and expected earnings of $2.

12. STU stock just paid a dividend of $1.50. Dividends are expected to grow at a rate of 15% for three years and at a rate of 6% thereafter. If the market capitalization rate is 10% and the market price is equal to the intrinsic value, what is the current price of STU?

13. XYZ stock just paid a dividend of $2. Dividends are expected to grow at a 10% rate for five years and at a 5% rate thereafter. Calculate the intrinsic value of XYZ assuming the required rate of return is 11%.

14. What is the intrinsic value of a stock that just paid a dividend of $1.80 if the market capitalization rate is 14% and dividends are expected to grow at a 20% rate for two years, a 15% rate for the next two years, and a 6% rate thereafter?

15. ABC stock just paid a dividend of $2. The dividends are expected to grow at 30% next year, and the growth rate is expected to decline over 12 years to a constant 6%. If the required rate of return is 15%, what is the intrinsic value of ABC stock given by the H model?

16. What is the expected yield to maturity on the stock in Problem 15 if the current market price is $40?

17. Answer Problem 15 assuming the decline in the dividend growth rate takes place over 20 years.

18. Given the following information, calculate the intrinsic value of each stock.

Stock	Estimated Earnings	P/E Multiple
A	2.50	10
B	1.30	16
C	4.20	8

19. DEF Corporation has a pretax cash flow from operations of $5,000,000 and expects that this will grow by 5% per year forever. To achieve this growth, 12% of the pretax cash flow from operations will have to be invested. Depreciation was $450,000 and is expected to grow at the same rate as the operating cash flow. The appropriate market capitalization rate is 10%, and the tax rate is 30%. What is the value of the unlevered firm?

SOLUTIONS

1. 200,000,000/8,000,000 = $25/share

2. Liquidation value = .8(500,000,000) = 4,000,000
   Available to shareholders = 400,000,000 - 300,000,000 = 100,000,000
   100,000,000/8,000,000 = $12.50/share

3. Replacement cost of assets = 1.2(500,000,000) = 600,000,000
   less liabilities of 300,000,000 leaves 300,000,000 for shareholders
   300,000,000/8,000,000 = $37.50
   q = 40/37.5 = 1.067

4. a. Rate of price appreciation = $\frac{42.50 - 38.75}{38.75}$ = .0968

Dividend yields = 1.30/38.75 = .0335
HPR = .0968 + .0335 = .1303

b. .06 + .9(.06) = .114

c. V_o = (42.50 + 1.30)/1.114 = $39.32

The intrinsic value is above market price, so the investor should hold more DEF than a passive strategy would dictate.

5. K_A = .07 + .8(.10) = .15

K_B = .07 + 1.2(.10) = .19

K_C = .07 + 1.4(.10) = .21

K_D = .07 + 1.5(.10) = .22

$V_o(A)$ = (54.50 + 2.00)/1.15 = $49.13   include less

$V_o(B)$ = (41.00 + 1.15)/1.19 = $35.42   include more

$V_o(C)$ = (22.50 + 2.50)/1.21 = $20.66   include more

$V_o(D)$ = (47.25 + 1.40)/1.22 = $39.88   include less

6. a. V_o = 3(1.06)/(.13 - .06) = $45.43

b. V_o = 3.18/(.15 - .06) = $35.33

c. V_0 = 3.18/(.17 - .06) = $28.91

7. a. V_o = 2(1.04)/(.12 - .04) = $26.00

b. V_o = 2(1.08)/(.12 - .08) = $54.00

c. V_o = 2(1.10)/(.12 - .10) = $110.00

8. a. V_o = 2.50(1.06)/(.15 - .06) = $29.44

b. $E(D_1)$ = 2.50(1.06) = $2.65

$E(r)$ = 2.65/25.00 + .06 = .166

c. $E(P_1)$ = $E(V_1)$ = 29.44(1.06) = $31.21

$E(r)$ = 2.65/25.00 + (31.21 - 25.00)/25.00 = .354

9. a. V_o = 3.20(1.05)/(.14 - .05) = $37.33

b. $E(D_1)$ = 3.20(1.05) = $3.36

$$E(r) = 3.36/35.00 + .05 = .146$$

c. $E(P_1) = E(V_1) = 37.33(1.05) = \$39.20$

$$E(r) = 3.36/35.00 + (39.20 - 35.00)/35.00 = .216$$

10. $g_A = .5(.10) = .05$

    $g_B = .6(.10) = .06$

    $g_C = .6(.15) = .09$

    $g_D = .8(.15) = .12$

11. $V_o(A) = .5(2)/(.14 - .05) = \$11.11$

    $V_o(B) = .6(2)/(.14 - .06) = \$15.00$

    $V_o(C) = .6(2)/(.14 - .09) = \$24.00$

    $V_o(D) = .8(2)/(.14 - .12) = \$80.00$

12. $E(D_1) = 1.50(1.15) = \$1.73$

    $E(D_2) = 1.50(1.15)^2 = \$1.98$

    $E(D_3) = 1.50(1.15)^3 = \$2.28$

    $E(D_4) = 1.50(1.15)^3(1.06) = \$2.42$

    $E(P_3) = 2.42/(.10 - .06) = \$60.50$

    $P_o = 1.73/1.10 + 1.98/1.10^2 + (2.42 + 60.50)/1.10^3$

    $ = 1.57 + 1.64 + 47.27$

    $ = \$50.48$

13. $E(D_1) = 2(1.1) = \$2.20$

    $E(D_2) = 2(1.1)^2 = \$2.42$

    $E(D_3) = 2(1.1)^3 = \$2.66$

    $E(D_4) = 2(1.1)^4 = \$2.93$

    $E(D_5) = 2(1.1)^5 = \$3.22$

    $E(D_6) = 2(1.1)^5(1.05) = \$3.38$

    $E(P_5) = 3.38(.11 - .05) = \$56.33$

$$P_o = 2.20/1.1 + 2.42/1.1^2 + 2.66/1.1^3 + 2.93/1.1^4$$
$$+ (3.22 + 56.33)/1.1^5$$
$$= 1.98 + 1.96 + 1.94 + 1.93 + 35.34$$
$$= \$43.15$$

14. $E(D_1) = 1.8(1.2) = \$2.16$

    $E(D_2) = 1.8(1.2)^2 = \$2.59$

    $E(D_3) = 1.8(1.2)^2(1.15) = \$2.98$

    $E(D_4) = 1.8(1.2)^2(1.15)^2 = \$3.43$

    $E(D_5) = 1.8(1.2)^2(1.15)^2(1.06) = \$3.63$

    $E(P_4) = 3.63/(.14 - .06) = \$45.38$

    $P_o = 2.16/1.14 + 2.59/1.14^2 + 2.98/1.14^3 + (3.43 + 45.38)/1.14^4$

    $= 1.89 + 1.99 + 2.01 + 28.90$

    $= \$34.79$

15. $P_o = \dfrac{2(1.06)}{.15 - .06} + \dfrac{2(6)(.30 - .06)}{.15 - .06}$

    $= 23.56 + 32.00$
    $= \$55.56$

16. $y = 2/40\,[1.06 + 6(.30 - .06)] + .06$

    $= .185$

17. $P_o = \dfrac{2(1.06)}{.15 - .06} + \dfrac{2(10)(.30 - .06)}{.15 - .06}$

    $= 23.56 + 53.33$
    $= \$76.89$

18. $V_o(A) = 2.5(10) = \$25.00$

    $V_o(B) = 1.3(16) = \$20.80$

    $V_o(C) = 4.2(8) = \$33.60$

19. Next year

Before-tax cash flow from operations	$5,250,000
Depreciation	472,500
Taxable income	4,777,500

Taxes	1,433,250
After-tax unleveraged income	3,344,250
After-tax cash flow from operations	3,816,750
New investment	630,000
Free cash flow	2,556,750

$V_o = 2,556,750/(.10 - .05) = \$51,135,000$

18 Fundamental Analysis

OUTLINE

I. Earnings

    A. Accounting earnings vs. economic earnings

    B. Earnings and stock price

        1. Price reaction to earnings announcements
        2. Forecasting earnings
        3. The value line system

II. Return on equity and financial leverage

III. Ratio analysis

    A. Decomposition of return on equity (ROE)

    B. Asset utilization ratios

    C. Liquidity and coverage ratios

    D. Market price ratios

IV. Comparability

    A. Inventory

    B. Depreciation

    C. Effects of inflation

V. The Graham technique

HIGHLIGHTS

    Reported earnings have been shown to be an important factor in explaining stock price behavior, but the security analyst is interested in the real earnings of the firm. Firms have a great deal of latitude in how various revenue and expense items are computed, so comparing different firms requires conversion of reported figures to a uniform standard. Inflation also presents problems for the analyst as it distorts the values of inventory, depreciation and interest expense. ROE is a primary determinant of the growth in earnings and is directly affected by the degree of financial leverage. A firm can increase return on equity (ROE) by borrowing as long as the interest rate is less than the return on assets (ROA). The firm's ROE can be broken down into profit margin, asset turnover and leverage ratios in order to more completely understand changes in ROE. In addition, useful information may be gained by computing asset utilization ratios, liquidity and coverage ratios, and market price ratios. Current values of these ratios are compared to past values of the ratios for the firm and to the values of these ratios for other firms in the industry to judge the financial health of the firm.

PROBLEMS

1. Given the following information, calculate ROE. The tax rate is 40%.

   a. ROA = 10%, debt/equity = 1, interest rate on debt = 11%
   b. ROA = 10%, debt/equity = 1.5, interest rate on debt = 11%
   c. ROA = 12%, debt/equity = 1.5, interest rate on debt = 9%
   d. ROA = 12%, debt/equity = 2, interest rate on debt = 9%

2. What is ROE in each of the following cases? The tax rate is 30%, and the interest rate is 12%.

   a. ROA = 8%, debt/equity = .8
   b. ROA = 8%, debt/equity = 1.4
   c. ROA = 15%, debt/equity = .6
   d. ROA = 15%, debt/equity = 1.2

Use the following information for Problems 3-15

Income Statements	1985	1986	1987
Sales	250,000	287,500	330,625
Cost of goods sold (including depreciation)	110,000	126,500	145,475
Depreciation	30,000	34,500	39,675
Selling and administrative expenses	40,000	48,000	57,000
Operating income	70,000	78,500	88,475
Interest expense	45,000	55,800	68,400
Taxable income	25,000	22,700	20,075
Income tax	10,000	9,080	8,030
Net income	15,000	13,620	12,045

Balance Sheets (end of year)	1984	1985	1986	1987
Cash and marketable securities	100,000	115,000	132,500	152,100
Accounts receivable	50,000	57,000	65,420	80,625
Inventories	150,000	165,000	181,500	199,600
Net plant and equipment	300,000	340,000	385,000	430,000
Total assets	600,000	677,000	764,420	862,335
Accounts payable	80,000	92,000	105,800	121,670
Short-term debt	100,000	150,000	210,000	280,000
Long-term debt (10% bonds maturing in 1990)	180,000	180,000	180,000	180,000
Total liabilities	360,000	422,000	495,800	581,670
Shareholder's equity	240,000	255,000	268,620	280,665

There are 30,000 shares of stock outstanding and the market price of the stock at year end was $15 in 1985, $13 in 1986, and $11 in 1987.

3. Calculate the ratio of net profit/pretax profit for each of the last three years.

4. Calculate the ratio of pretax profit/EBIT for each of the last three years.

5. What is the leverage ratio for each of the last three years?

6. What is the asset turnover ratio for each of the last three years?

7. What is the fixed asset turnover ratio for each of the last three years?

8. Calculate the profit margin for each of the last three years.

9. Calculate the current ratio for each of the last three years.

10. Calculate the quick ratio for each of the last three years.

11. What is the days receivable for each of the last three years?

12. What is the interest coverage ratio for each of the last three years?

13. Calculate the market to book ratio for each of the last three years.

14. Calculate the price/earnings ratio for each of the last three years.

15. What is the ROE for each of the last three years? What appears to be causing the change in ROE?

SOLUTIONS

1. a. ROE = (1 − .4)[.10 + (.10 − .11) 1]   = .054
   b. ROE = (1 − .4)[.10 + (.10 − .11) 1.5]   = .051
   c. ROE = (1 − .4)[.12 + (.12 − .09) 1.5]   = .099
   d. ROE = (1 − .4)[.12 + (.12 − .09) 2]   = .108

2. a. ROE = (1 − .3)[.08 + (.08 − .12) .8]   = .0336
   b. ROE = (1 − .3)[.08 + (.08 − .12) 1.4]   = .0168

    c.   ROE = (1 - .3)[.15 + (.15 - .12) .6] = .1176
    d.   ROE = (1 - .3)[.15 + (.15 - .12) 1.2] = .1302

3.   1985   15,000/25,000 = .6
      1986   13,620/22,700 = .6
      1987   12,045/20,075 = .6

4.   1985   25,000/70,000 = .357
      1986   22,700/78,500 = .289
      1987   20,075/88,475 = .227

5.   1985   677,000/255,000 = 2.655
      1986   764,420/268,620 = 2.846
      1987   862,335/280,665 = 3.072

6.   1985   250,000/[(600,000 + 677,000)/2] = .392
      1986   287,500/[(677,000 + 764,420)/2] = .399
      1987   330,625/[(764,420 + 862,335)/2] = .406

7.   1985   250,000/[(300,000 + 340,000)/2] = .781
      1986   287,500/[(340,000 + 385,000)/2] = .793
      1987   330,625/[(385,000 + 430,000)/2] = .811

8.   1985   70,000/250,000 = .28
      1986   78,500/287,500 = .273
      1987   88,475/330,625 = .268

9.   1985 (115,000 + 57,000 + 165,000)/(92,000 + 150,000) = 1.393
      1986 (132,500 + 65,420 + 181,500)/(105,800 + 210,000) = 1.201
      1987 (152,100 + 80,625 + 199,600)/(121,670 + 280,000) = 1.076

10. 1985 (115,000 + 57,000)/242,000 = .711
      1986 (132,500 + 65,420)/315,800 = .627
      1987 (152,100 + 80,625)/401,670 = .579

11. 1985   250,000/[(50,000 + 57,000)/2] = 4.673
      1986   287,500/[(57,000 + 65,420)/2] = 4.697
      1987   330,625/[(65,420 + 80,625)/2] = 4.528

12. 1985   70,000/45,000 = 1.556
      1986   78,500/55,800 = 1.407
      1987   88,475/68,400 = 1.293

13. 1985   15/(255,000/30,000) = 1.765
      1986   13/(268,620/30,000) = 1.452
      1987   11/(280,665/30,000) = 1.176

14. 1985   15/(15,000/30,000) = 30
      1986   13/(13,620/30,000) = 28.63
      1987   11/(12,045/30,000) = 27.4

15. 1985   15,000/255,000 = .059
     1986   13,620/268,620 = .051
     1987   12,045/280,665 = .043

The ROE is declining because of the extensive use of high-cost, short-term debt. The rate of interest exceeds the return on assets, and thus ROE declines as the firm becomes more leveraged. The asset turnover ratios reveal the firm is producing sales with the same efficiency.

19 An Introduction to Options Markets

OUTLINE

I. The stock option contract
   A. Terms of the contract
   B. Adjustment of the contract

II. Other option contracts
   A. Index options
   B. Foreign currency options
   C. Futures options

III. Values of options at expiration
   A. Call
   B. Put
   C. Option vs. stock investment
   D. Put-call parity

IV. Combinations of options
   A. Protective put
   B. Covered call
   C. Straddle
   D. Spread

V. Option valuation
   A. Determinants of option value
   B. The Black/Scholes formula

VI. Bull and bear CDs.

HIGHLIGHTS

A call option allows the holder to buy an asset at an agreed-upon price, while a put option allows the holder to sell an asset an an agreed-upon price. A European option may only be exercised at maturity, while an American option may be exercised at any time, up to and including maturity. The holder of an option cannot lose more than the premium paid for the option, and if stock price moves in the correct direction, options offer a greater return than an investment in the stock. The volume of option contracts grew dramatically with the standardization of option contracts and exchange trading. Options are currently traded on a variety of instruments other than common stock. A call option is more valuable the lower the exercise price, the longer the time to maturity, the higher the stock price, the higher the risk-free rate, the greater the underlying asset volatility, and the lower the dividend payout. Since option values are based on the value of some other asset, a specific relationship known as put-call parity exists between the price of a call option and an identical put option. If put-call parity is violated, arbitrage opportunities will exist and market forces will force parity. Strategies involving combinations of options or options and the underlining asset allow the investor to either increase or decrease risk and to control the amount and direction of that risk.

PROBLEMS

1. What is the profit per share to the holder of a call option with a $40.00 exercise price if it cost $3 and the stock price at expiration is
   a. $30?
   b. $40?
   c. $50?
   d. $75?

2. Calculate the profit per share to the holder of a call option with a $45 exercise price if it cost $2.50 and the stock price at expiration is

a. $40?
   b. $45?
   c. $47.50?
   d. $50?

3. Calculate the profit per share to the holder of a put option with an exercise price of $90, assuming the option cost $5.20 and the stock price at expiration is
   a. $110?
   b. $90?
   c. $43.75?
   d. $0?

4. Calculate the profit per share to the holder of a put option with an exercise price of $45, assuming the option cost $6.25 and the stock price at expiration is
   a. $50.00.
   b. $45.00.
   c. $38.75.
   d. $36.25

5. What are the payoffs to the writers of the options in Problems 1-4?

6. ABC stock pays no dividends and is currently selling for $100/share. A six-month call option on ABC with an exercise price of $100 is selling for $5/share. You have $10,000 to invest, and the price of ABC in six-months will be $80, $90, $100, $110, or $120. Calculate the returns from both the stock and option strategies.

7. Using the information in Problem 6, calculate the returns to the portfolios that place the following percentages in six-month T-bills that earn 4% over the period and the remainder in options:
   a. 70%
   b. 80%
   c. 90%

8. Calculate the profit per share to purchasing DEF stock at $50 and a put with a $50 exercise price for $4, given the following stock prices at expiration:

a. $60
b. $50
c. $40
d. $30

9. Calculate the profit per share to purchasing GHI stock at $75 and a put option with a $75 exercise price for $5, given the following stock prices at expiration.
   a. $80
   b. $75
   c. $70
   d. $65

10. You purchase one share of JKL stock at $60 and write a call with a $65 exercise price for $3. What is your profit given the following stock prices at expiration?
    a. $55
    b. $60
    c. $65
    d. $70

11. You write a covered call with an exercise price of $80 on one share of MNO stock that you purchased at $80. If the premium is $4, what is the profit assuming the following stock prices hold at expiration?
    a. $73
    b. $77
    c. $80
    d. $85

12. Suppose you purchase a straddle with a $75 exercise price and the call costs $5 and the put costs $4. Calculate your profit given the following stock prices at expiration:
    a. $84
    b. $75
    c. $66
    d. $50

13. What are the break-even points from purchasing a $60 straddle if the call option costs $3.50 and the put costs $2.75?

14. Calculate the maximum profit and maximum loss from purchasing a call with an exercise price of $95 for $7.50 and selling a call on the same stock with the same expiration with an exercise price of $100 for $6.

15. Given the following information, calculate the Black/Sholes price for the call option:

    Stock price = $40
    Exercise price = $45
    Risk-free rate = .06
    Time to maturity = .25 year
    Standard deviation = .3

16. What is the Black/Sholes price of a put option on the same stock with a $45 exercise price?

17. Answer Problem 15 assuming the stock price is $43.

18. Answer Problem 15 assuming the exercise price is $50.

19. Answer Problem 15 assuming the risk-free rate is .08.

20. Answer Problem 15 assuming the time to maturity is .16 year.

21. Answer Problem 15 assuming the standard deviation is .4.

SOLUTIONS

1. Profit = value of the option - premium

   a. 0 - 3 = -$3
   b. 0 - 3 = -$3
   c. 10 - 3 = $7
   d. 35 - 3 = $32

2. a. 0   - 2.50 = -$2.50
   b. 0   - 2.50 = -$2.50
   c. 2.50 - 2.50 = $0
   d. 5.00 - 2.50 = $2.50

3. Profit = value of the option - premium

   a. 0   - 5.20 = -$5.20
   b. 0   - 5.20 = -$5.20
   c. 46.25 - 5.20 = $41.05
   d. 90   - 5.20 = $84.80

4. a. 0   - 6.25 = -$6.25
   b. 0   - 6.25 = -$6.25
   c. 6.25 - 6.25 = $0
   d. 8.75 - 6.25 = $2.50

5. The profit to the writer of the option is the negative of the profit to the holder. Options are a zero-sum game: whatever one party gains, the other party loses.

6. With $10,000 you can purchase 2000 options or 100 shares of stock.

Stock Price	Value of Options	Value of Stock
$80	0	$8,000
$90	0	$9,000
$100	0	$10,000
$110	$20,000	$11,000
$120	$40,000	$12,000

Stock Price	Return to Options	Return to Stock
$80	-100%	-20%
$90	-100%	-10%
$100	-100%	0
$110	100%	10%
$120	300%	20%

7. Placing 70% of your wealth in T-bills allows you to purchase 600 options. The T-bill will return 7000(1.04) = $7280.

Placing 80% of your wealth in T-bills allows you to purchase 400 options. The T-bills will return 8000(1.04) = $8320.

Placing 90% of your wealth in T-bills allows you to purchase 200 options. The T-bills will return 9000(1.04) = $9360.

The value of each portfolio is the sum of the value of the T-bills and the value of the options.

Stock Price	Value of 70% Port	Value of 80% Port	Value of 90% Port
$80	$7,280	$8,320	$9,360
$90	$7,280	$8,320	$9,360
$100	$7,280	$8,320	$9,360
$110	$13,280	$12,320	$11,360
$120	$19,280	$16,320	$13,360

Stock Price	Return to 70% Port	Return to 80% Port	Return to 90% Port
$80	-27.2%	-16.8%	-6.4%
$90	-27.2%	-16.8%	-6.4%
$100	-27.2%	-16.8%	-6.4%
$110	32.8%	23.2%	13.6%
$120	92.8%	63.2%	33.6%

8. Profit = profit from stock + value of the option - premium

    a. 10 + 0 - 4 = $6
    b.   0 + 0 - 4 = -$4
    c. -10 + 10 - 4 = -$4
    d. -20 + 20 - 4 = -$4

9.   a.   5 + 0 - 5 = $0
    b.   0 + 0 - 5 = -$5
    c. -5 + 5 - 5 = -$5
    d. -10 + 10 - 5 = -$5

10. Profit = profit from stock - value of the option + premium

    a. -5 - 0 + 3 = -$2
    b.   0 - 0 + 3 = $3
    c.   5 - 0 + 3 = $8
    d. 10 - 5 + 3 = $8

11. a. -7 - 0 + 4 = $3
    b. -3 - 0 + 4 = $1
    c.   0 - 0 + 4 = $4
    d.   5 - 5 + 4 = $4

12. Profit = value of call + value of put - call premium - put premium

a. $9 + 0 - 5 - 4 = \$0$
b. $0 + 0 - 5 - 4 = -\$9$
c. $0 + 9 - 5 - 4 = \$0$
d. $0 + 25 - 5 - 4 = \$16$

13. Total premium to cover = $3.50 + 2.75 = \$6.25$
    Break-even: $60 + 6.25 = \$66.25$
    $60 - 6.25 = \$53.75$

14. The maximum profit occurs when stock price is above the higher exercise price.
    Profit = $(100 - 95) + (6.00 - 7.50) = \$3.50$

15. $d_1 = \dfrac{\log(40/45) + (.06 + .09/2).25}{.3(.5)} = -.61$

    $d_2 = -.61 - .3(.5) = -.76$

    $N(d_1) = .2710$

    $N(d_2) = .2236$

    $C = 40(.2710) - 45(.985)(.2236) = \$.93$

16. $P = .93 - 40 + 45(.985)$ by put-call parity
    $= \$5.26$

17. $d_1 = \dfrac{\log(43/45) + (.06 + .09/2).25}{.3(.5)} = -.13$

    $d_2 = -.13 - .3(.5) = -.28$

    $N(d_1) = .4483$

    $N(d_2) = .3897$

    $C = 43(.4483) - 45(.985)(.3897) = \$2.00$

18. $d_1 = \dfrac{\log(40/50) + (.06 + .09/2).25}{.3(.5)} = -1.31$

    $d_2 = -1.31 - .3(.5) = -1.46$

    $N(d_1) = .0951$

    $N(d_2) = .0721$

    $C = 40(.0951) - 50(.985)(.0721) = \$.25$

19. $d_1 = \dfrac{\log(40/45) + (.08 + .09/2).25}{.3(.5)} = -.58$

$d_2 = -.58 - .3(.5) = -.73$

$N(d_1) = .2810$

$N(d_2) = .2328$

$C = 40(.2810) - 45(.980)(.2328) = \$.97$

20. $d_1 = \dfrac{\ln(40/45) + (.06 + .09/2).16}{.3(.4)} = -.84$

$d_2 = -.84 - .3(.4) = -.96$

$N(d_1) = .2005$

$N(d_2) = .1685$

$C = 40(.2005) - 45(.990)(.1685) = \$.51$

21. $d_1 = \dfrac{\ln(40/45) + (.06 + .16/2).25}{.4(.5)} = -.41$

$d_2 = -.41 - .4(.5) = -.61$

$N(d_1) = .3410$

$N(d_2) = .2710$

$C = 40(.3410) - 45(.985)(.2710) = \$1.63$

20 Options Markets: A Closer Look

OUTLINE

I. Additional factors in option pricing
   A. Restrictions on the value of a call option
   B. Early exercise and dividends
   C. Dividends and call valuation
   D. Dividends and put valuation

II. Hedge ratios
   A. The Black/Scholes formula
   B. Portfolio insurance

III. Option-like securities
   A. Callable bonds
   B. Convertible securities
   C. Warrants
   D. Collateralized loans
   E. Leveraged equity

IV. The binomial option pricing model
   A. Two periods
   B. More than two periods

V. Empirical evidence on option pricing

HIGHLIGHTS

The Black/Scholes formula is derived for European options, but it is also valid for American call options on non-dividend-paying stocks. This is because the option is worth more alive than dead. The model is not valid for deriving the value of an American put, because there are instances when early exercise is optimal. The introduction of dividends raises the possibility of optimal early exercise of an American call, and more complex valuation models are needed. The hedge ratio is the number of shares of stock needed to hedge the price risk of writing one option. The elasticity of an option is greater than one; the price of an option will change by a larger percentage than the percentage change in stock price. Portfolio insurance is obtained by purchasing a put option if it is available, or by creating a synthetic put by selling a specific fraction of the equity portfolio and putting the proceeds in risk-free assets. Securities such as callable bonds and convertible bonds, as well as other financial arrangements, represent options and may be analyzed within the option pricing framework. The Black/Scholes model may be interpreted as the limiting case of the binomial optional pricing model, where the number of periods gets very large and the possible change in stock price in any period gets very small.

PROBLEMS

1. Compute the psuedo-American call value for a stock that is expected to pay a $2 dividend in .16 year given the following information:

   Risk-free rate = .08
   Current stock price = $45
   Exercise price = $50
   Time to maturity of option = .25 year
   Standard deviation = .3

2. Answer Problem 1 assuming the dividend is expected to be $4.

3. Answer Problem 1 assuming the current stock price is $55.

4. Consider a non-dividend-paying stock. Compute the hedge ratio for a call given the following information:

   Risk-free rate = .06
   Current stock price = $40
   Exercise price = $35
   Time to maturity = .36 year
   Standard deviation = .4

5. What is the hedge ratio for a put option, using the information in Problem 4?

6. Answer Problem 4 assuming the current stock price is $30.

7. What is the hedge ratio for a put, using the information in Problem 6?

8. Assume you write the call in Problem 5. If stock price increases by $3, what will be the change in the value of the option?

9. Assume you write the put in Problem 7. If stock price increases by $3, what will be the change in the value of the option?

10. What is the elasticity of a call option currently selling for $3 with an exercise price of $40 and hedge ratio = .7 if the stock price is currently $37?

11. Calculate the elasticity of a put option currently selling for $4 with an exercise price of $50 and hedge ratio = -.3 if the stock price is currently $60.

12. If you currently own an equity portfolio worth $450,000,000, how much equity must you sell off to synthetically create a protected put position if an at-the-money put would have a delta = -.4?

13. Assume that over the next period stock price can increase or decrease 20%. The current stock price is $40 and the risk-free rate is 10%. What is the price of a call option with an exercise price of $45?

14. Answer Problem 13 assuming stock price can increase or decrease by 30%.

15. Answer Problem 13 assuming the exercise price is $40.

CFA PROBLEMS

16. (CFA Examination 1987, Level III) You are considering the sale of a call option with an exercise price of $100 and one year to expiration. The underlying stock pays no dividends, its current price is $100, and you believe it has a 50% chance of increasing to $120 and a 50% chance of decreasing to $80. The risk-free rate of interest is 10%.

    a. Describe the specific steps involved in applying the binomial option pricing model to calculate the call option's value.

    b. Compare the binomial option pricing model to the Black-Scholes option pricing model.

17. (CFA Examination 1987, Level III) On June 1, 1987, an institutional portfolio manager is mananging a $1 million portfolio consisting of U.S. government bonds. Currently the portfolio is fully invested in one bond issue--government 8% bonds due June 1, 2002, selling at a market price of $100.

   The manager is concerned about the outlook for interest rates over the next months. The manager believes interest rates will move significantly with probabilities favoring a strong rise in rates, but a strong decline is also possible. For the next six-month holding period the manager's goal is to structure a portfolio which will be substantially protected from a rate rise, but which will also participate in any market advances.

   Other available investment instruments are the following:

   (1) <u>Futures contract</u> on government 8% bonds due 6/1/02

Futures expiration	12/1/87
Futures current price	$101
Contract size	$100,000

   (2) <u>Options contracts</u> on government 8% bonds due 6/1/02 expiring 12/1/87

Option	Strike Price	Market Price	Contract Size
Calls	100	4	$100,000
Puts	100	2	$100,000

   (3) <u>Treasury bills</u> maturing 12/1/87, yielding 3% for the six months

   a. Assume that the manager wishes to maintain the current bond holding. Design an option strategy that will achieve the manager's goal of protecting against an interest rate rise while also participating in any market advances.

   b. Assume that the manager is willing to maintain or sell the current bond holding. With the available instruments listed above, design two alternative portfolio structures which accomplish the same goal.

   c. Based upon the put-call parity relationship shown below, calculate which of the two strategies designed in Part b should be implemented.

   put price = call price - bond + present value of exercise price

   d. Comment on how the theory of option pricing can be used to develop a dynamic asset allocation strategy that protects this portfolio from downside returns. Comment on how such a strategy is executed.

18. (CFA Examination 1985, Level III) You have been asked to provide information concerning the use of the following option/futures strategies to modify portfolio risk/return relationships:

   a. Writing covered calls
   b. Purchasing protective puts (the long stock, long put strategy)
   c. Selling stock market futures

   Briefly describe each of these three strategies.

SOLUTIONS

1. Assuming early exercise

   $$d_1 = \frac{\log(45/50) + (.08 + .09/2)(.16)}{.3(.4)} = -.71$$

   $d_2 = -.71 - .12 = -.83$

   $N(d_1) = .2389$

   $N(d_2) = .2033$

   $C = 45(.2389) - 50(.987)(.2033) = \$.72$

   Adjusting stock price

   $$d_1 = \frac{\log(43.03/50) + (.08 + .09/2).25}{.3(.5)} = -.79$$

   $d_2 = -.79 - .15 = -.94$

   $N(d_1) = .2148$

   $N(d_2) = .1736$

   $C = 43.03(.2148) - 50(.980)(.1736) = \$.74$

   Call value is the lesser of the two or $.72.

2. Assuming early exercise, $C = \$.72$

   Adjusting stock price

   $$d_1 = \frac{\log(41.05/50) + (.08 + .09/2).25}{.3(.5)} = -1.11$$

   $d_2 = -.1.11 - .15 = -1.26$

   $N(d_1) = .1335$

   $N(d_2) = .1038$

   $C = 41.05(.1335) - 50(.980)(.1038) = \$.39$

   Price of the call = $.39

3. Assuming early exercise

$$d_1 = \frac{\log(55/50) + (.08 + .09/2).16}{.3(.4)} = .96$$

$$d_2 = .96 - .12 = .84$$

$$N(d_1) = .8315$$

$$N(d_2) = .7996$$

$$C = 55(.8315) - 50(.987)(.7996) = \$6.27$$

Adjusting stock price

$$d_1 = \frac{\log(53.03/50) + (.08 + .09/2).25}{.3(.5)} = .60$$

$$d_2 = .60 - .15 = .45$$

$$N(d_1) = .7258$$

$$N(d_2) = .6737$$

$$C = 53.03(.7258) - 50(.980)(.6737) = \$5.48$$

Price = \$5.48

4. Hedge ratio = $N(d_1)$

$$d_1 = \frac{\log(40/35) + (.06 + .16/2).36}{.4(.6)} = .77$$

$$N(d_1) = .7794$$

5. Hedge ratio = $N(d_1) - 1 = .7794 - 1 = -.2206$

6. Hedge ratio = $N(d_1)$

$$d_1 = \frac{\log(30/35) + (.06 + .16/2).36}{.4(.6)} = -.43$$

$$N(d_1) = .3336$$

7. Hedge ratio = $N(d_1) - 1 = .3336 - 1 = -.6664$

8. Change in value of call = $.3336 \times 3 = \$1$

9. Change in value of put = $-.6664 \times 3 = -\$2$

10. Change in value of call = .70

    Percentage change in value of call = .70/3 = 23.3%

    Percentage change in value of stock = 1/37 = 2.7%

    Elasticity = 23.3/2.7 = 8.63

11. Change in value of put = -.30

    Percentage change in value of put = -.30/4 = -7.5%

    Percentage change in value of stock = 1/60 = 1.7%

    Elasticity = -7.5/1.7 = -4.41

12. You need to sell 40% or $180,000,000.

13. At the end of the period the stock price will be 40(1.2) = $48 and the call will be worth $3, or the stock price will be 40(.8) = $32 and the call will be worth $0. The hedge ratio is (3 - 0)/(48 - 32) = 3/16. A portfolio with one written call and 3/16 share will be worth $6 with certainty. The current value of this portfolio is $6/1.1 = $5.45. Solving $3/16\ S_o - C_o = 5.45$, the value of the call is $2.05.

14. The hedge ratio is (7 - 0)/(52 - 27) = 7/25. A portfolio with one written call and 7/25 share will be worth $7.56 with certainty. The current value of this portfolio is 7.56/1.1 = $6.87. Solving $7/25\ S_o - C_o = 6.87$, the value of the call is $4.33.

15. The hedge ratio is (8 - 0)/(48 - 32) = .5. A portfolio with one written call and .5 share of stock will be worth $16 with certainty. The current value of this portfolio is 16/1.1 = $14.55. Solving $.5\ S_o - C_o = 14.55$, the value of the call is $5.45.

16. a. Hedge ratio = $\dfrac{C_u - C_d}{uS - dS} = \dfrac{20 - 0}{120 - 80} = .5$

    Implied probability (p) = $\dfrac{(1 + r) - d}{u - d} = \dfrac{(1.1) - .8}{1.2 - .8} = .75$

    Call value = $\dfrac{pC_u + (1 - p)C_d}{1 + r} = \dfrac{.75(20) + .25(0)}{1.1} = 13.6$

    Or

Step 1

Set up a binomial tree and calculate the option values at expiration for each ending stock price.

Step 2

Solve for the amount to invest in the stock and the amount to borrow in order to replicate the option given its value in the up state and its value in the down state. Solve these equations simultaneously.

Step 3

Use the values derived in Step 2 to solve for the value of the option at the beginning of the period.

Or

Step 1

```
                120
                (C = 20)
    100
                 80
                (C = 0)
```

Step 2

$20 = 120*D - 1.1*B$
$0 = 80*D - 1.1*B$

$D = \dfrac{-1.1(20) - (-1.1)0}{120(-1.1) - 80(-1.1)} = \dfrac{-22}{-44} = .5$

$C = 80(.5) - 1.1*B$

$0 = 80(.5) - 1.1*B$

$B = 40/1.1 = 36.4$

Step 3

$C = 50 - 36.4 = 13.6$

b. The binomial option pricing model is a discrete version of the continuous time Black-Scholes option pricing model. As the number of intervals in the binomial model approaches infinity, the option value derived from this model approaches the option value derived from the Black-Scholes model.

The binomial model is more flexible than the Black-Scholes model because it does not require one to assume constant interest rates and constant variance throughout the horizon. These values can be changed at any of the nodes in the binomial tree. However, the binomial model is more cumbersome to use since accuracy requires that the tree include many nodes.

17. a. The manager wishes to be protected from any decline in the government bonds' price (any rise in rates) while maintaining a participation in a price advance, should it occur. The manager also wishes to hold the existing bond position over the next six months. The option strategy best suited for this goal is a <u>protected put strategy</u>.

    The manager should purchase the put options in a quantity sufficient to protect the $1.0 million portfolio. The manager should purchase <u>10</u> put contracts. In this strategy, the bond portfolio will be protected against any price decline below 98, (the put strike price less the put premium) yet will participate with any price advance on the bond less 2.00 (the put premium).

    b. The manager is now willing to sell the existing bonds in order to create a portfolio structure that achieves the goal. Two strategic options structures equivalent to the structure in Part a above can be designed as follows:

    <u>Alternative 1</u>

    - Sell the 8% government bonds.
    - Invest the proceeds in the T-bills and buy the appropriate amount of 8% bond futures.
    - Buy the put options to protect against price declines while participating in price advances.

    Buying T-bills and futures is equivalent to holding the bonds. The manager could purchase $1 million in T-bills and <u>10</u> futures contracts.

    The manager would complete the option strategy Alternative 1 by buying 10 put options.

    <u>Alternative 2</u>

    - Sell the 8% government bonds.
    - Invest the proceeds in the T-bills.
    - Buy the appropriate amount of call options.

    A T-bill plus call option position is equivalent in structure to a bond plus put option position. The bill plus call option provides protection against bond price declines since the investor can only lose the premium on the call option. Participation in any bond price advance is achieved since the call option premium will increase.

Specifically, the manager could purchase $1 million in T-bills and <u>10</u> call options.

c. Given the put-call parity pricing relationship, the put options and call options appear misvalued versus each other.

If the call is correctly priced at 4, the put should be priced at:

Put = 4 - bond price = present value of strike price
    = 4 - 100 + 100/1.03
    = 4 - 100 + 97.09
    = 1.09

If the put is correctly priced at 2, the call should be priced at:

Call = 2 + 100 - 100/1.03
     = 2 + 100 - 97.09
     = 4.91

The put is <u>overpriced</u> versus the call. Therefore:

(1) In the put buying strategies the put premium appears very fully priced.
(2) In the future buying/put buying strategy, similar comments hold. Also the future appears <u>overvalued</u>.
(3) In the buy bills/buy calls strategy, the call option price appears attractive.

In addition, the price of the future at 101 appears high; a fair price for the future would be:

Price future = price bond + (bill income - bond income)
     Price = 100 + (- 1)
           = 99

The option strategy involving buying T-bills and the call options is recommended.

d. It is possible to replicate a protective put strategy based on the theory of option pricing but without actual investment in options. Such a strategy would have the effect of limiting a portfolio's downside return.

The strategy calls for the continual rebalancing of a portfolio between a risky asset and a riskless asset. In this case, the risky asset would be long-term government bonds while the riskless asset would be T-bills or money market instruments. The particular percentage to be allocated to the risky and riskless components is determined from the option pricing formula.

18. a. Writing covered calls -- This strategy involves the purchase of common shares and the simultaneous writing (selling) of call options on that stock with the intent of earning the time value premium on the call options. A call option allows the call holder to purchase the stock at a guaranteed price, the strike price, over a limited period of time.

b. Purchasing protective puts (long stock, long put) -- This strategy entails the purchase of a put option(s) on a stock(s) held in the portfolio in order to protect against a significant decline in the prices of the respective stock(s). A put option allows the put holder the right to sell the stock to the put writer at a guaranteed price for a limited period of time.

c. Selling stock market index futures -- This strategy involves the selling of some stock market index futures (forward) contract (such as the S&P 500, NYSE Composite, Value Line Average, or S&P 100) while at the same time owning a diversified portfolio of common stocks in order to hedge against a decline in the general market or as a speculation that the market or common stocks will decline.

Chapter 21 Futures and Forward Markets: General Principles

OUTLINE

I. Futures and forward contracts

   A. Basics

   B. Types of contracts

II. Trading in futures markets

   A. The clearing house and open interest

   B. Marking to market and the margin account

   C. Cash delivery vs. actual delivery

   D. Regulation

   E. Taxation

III. Futures markets strategies

   A. Hedging vs. speculating

   B. Basis risk and the imperfect hedge

IV. Determination of futures prices

   A. Spot - futures parity

   B. Spread parity

   C. Futures prices vs. forward prices

V. Futures prices vs. expected spot prices

   A. Expectations hypothesis

   B. Normal backwardation

   C. Contango

   D. Modern portfolio theory

HIGHLIGHTS

Forward and futures contracts obligate the long trader to take delivery and the short trader to make delivery of a good at a time in the future at a currently established price. Futures contracts differ from forward contracts in that futures contracts call for daily settlement of profits and losses while forward contracts call for no payment until the contract expires. Also, futures contracts are traded on exchanges and are standardized as to delivery date, delivery location, size of the contract, and the good that is to be delivered. The clearing house is the intermediary between the long trader and short trader and guarantees performance. Traders can be separated into hedgers, who use the contract to get rid of risk, and speculators, who bet on future price. The futures market is a zero-sum game: whatever the long position gains the short position loses. In a normal market, the futures price will exceed the spot price by the cost of carrying the asset until maturity. The futures price will be less than the expected spot price if the spot price exhibits systematic risk. This is necessary to compensate the long position for the risk borne.

PROBLEMS

1. What are the profits to the long and short positions if the contracted price for corn is $2.40 and the price at maturity is $2.60? Assume four contracts.

2. Answer Problem 1 assuming the price at maturity is $2.15.

3. Illustrate the mark-to-market settlements for the long position for one corn contract if the futures price follows this pattern:

Day	Futures Price
0 (contract date)	$2.30
1	$2.40
2	$2.35
3	$2.30
4 (delivery)	$2.20

4. Illustrate the mark-to-market settlements for the long position for one corn contract if, futures price follows this pattern:

Day	Futures Price
0 (contract date)	$2.60
1	$2.50
2	$2.55
3	$2.65
4 (delivery)	$2.75

5. What is the profit to purchasing one S&P 500 index contract at 235 if the price at expiration is 241? The cost of the contract is 500 times the index value.

6. What is the profit to selling one S&P 500 index contract at 224 if the price at expiration is 217?

7. Consider a non-dividend-paying stock with a current price of $50. If the risk-free rate is .5% per month, what is the futures price for four-month delivery?

8. Using the information in Problem 7, what would be the arbitrage profit if the futures price were $52?

9. Using the information in Problem 7, what would be the arbitrage profit if the futures price were $50.50?

10. Consider a stock with a 5% annual dividend yield. If the T-bill rate is 10% and the current stock price is $70, what is the futures price for one-year delivery?

11. Answer Problem 10 assuming the stock has a 7% dividend yield.

12. If the T-bill rate is 8% and the price of a January future on a stock with a 3% dividend yield is $100, what is the price of a July future?

13. What is the price of an April future on the stock in Problem 12?

14. What is the price of an October future on the stock in Problem 12?

SOLUTIONS

1. The long position promises to purchase the commodity, and in this case makes $.20/bushel. Each corn contract is for 5000 bushels, so the total profit to the long position is $.20(5000)(4) = $4000. The short position loses $4000.

2. The long position loses $.25/bushel for a total loss of $.25(5000)(4) = $5000. The short position makes a profit of $5000.

3.

Day	Profit per Bushel	x 5000 Bushels/Contract	Daily Proceeds
1	2.40 - 2.30 = .10		$500
2	2.35 - 2.40 = -.05		-$250
3	2.30 - 2.35 = -.05		-$250
4	2.20 - 2.30 = -.10		-$500
			-$500

4.

Day	Profit per Bushel	x 5000 Bushels/Contract	Daily Proceeds
1	2.50 - 2.60 = -.10		-$500
2	2.55 - 2.50 = .05		$250
3	2.65 - 2.55 = .10		$500
4	2.75 - 2.65 = .10		$500
			$1250

5. Profit = $(S_T - F_o)500$

   = (241 - 235)500
   = $3000

6. Profit = $(F_0 - S_T)500$

   $= (224 - 217)500$
   $= \$3500$

7. $F_0 = S_0(1 + r_f)^t$

   $= 50(1.005)^4$
   $= \$51.01$

8. The arbitrage strategy is as follows.

Action	CF, t = 0	CF, t = 4
Borrow $50	50	$-50(1.005)^4 = -\$51.01$
Buy stock for $50	-50	S_T
Enter short futures position (F = 52)	0	$52 - S_T$
total	0	$.99

   A riskless profit of $.99 can be made.

9. The arbitrage strategy is the reverse of the strategy in Problem 8.

Action	CF, t = 0	CF, t = 4
Invest $50	50	$-50(1.005)^4 = \$51.01$
Short stock for $50	50	$-S_T$
Enter long futures position (F = 50.50)	0	$S_T - 50.50$
Total	0	$.49

10. $F_0 = S_0(1 + r_f - d)^T$

    $= 70(1 + .10 - .05)$

    $= \$73.50$

11. $F_0 = 70(1 + .10 - .07)$

    $= \$72.10$

12. $F_{July} = 100(1 + .08 - .03)^{.5}$
    $= \$102.47$

13. $F_{April} = 100(1 + .08 - .03)^{.25}$
    $= \$101.23$

14. $F_{October} = 100(1 + .08 - .03)^{.75}$
    $= \$103.73$

22 Futures Markets: A Closer Look

OUTLINE

I. Stock index futures

    A. The contracts

    B. Synthetic stock positions

    C. Empirical pricing evidence

    D. Index arbitrage

II. Foreign exchange futures

    A. The markets

    B. Interest rate parity

III. Interest rate futures

IV. Commodity futures

    A. Pricing with storage costs

    B. Pricing using discounted cash flow analysis

V. New futures contracts

    A. The CPI contract

    B. Other contracts

HIGHLIGHTS

Futures are traded on several stock market indices. Index futures may be used along with T-bills to create synthetic equity positions. The payoffs to these positions are identical to the stock position, but the positions may be opened and closed at much lower transaction costs. Program trading attempts to exploit violations of parity between the index spot price and the futures price. Futures are traded on several foreign currencies, and an informal forward market also exists in foreign currencies. Futures prices on currencies are determined by interest rate parity. Interest rate futures allow one to speculate on, or hedge against, interest rate fluctuations. Commodities that are stored by investors may be priced as though they pay a negative dividend. Instead of receiving a dividend, the investor holding the asset must pay for storage or carrying costs. Future markets arise from a desire to hedge risk. As new hedging demands are perceived, futures contracts will be designed to meet those needs.

PROBLEMS

1. Calculate the parity price of a six-month S&P future if the risk-free rate is 4% semiannually, the dividend yield over the next six months is expected to be 2%, and the index currently has a value of 280.

2. Answer Problem 1 assuming the risk-free rate is 5% semiannually.

3. Answer Problem 1 assuming the estimated dividend yield doubles.

4. Calculate the futures parity price (in dollars) for a one-year British pound contract if the spot price is $1.70 and the risk-free rates are .08 in the U.S. and .05 in the U.K.

5. Answer Problem 4 assuming the U.S. risk-free rate is .09.

6. Answer Problem 4 assuming the U.K. risk-free rate is .07.

7. What is the arbitrage profit if the futures price in Problem 4 is $1.72?

8. What is the arbitrage profit if the futures price in Problem 4 is $1.76?

9. The risk-free rate is 8%. The current price of gold is $600/ounce. Determine the price of a one-year futures contract if carrying costs are 1% of the spot price.

10. Answer Problem 9 assuming carrying costs are 2% of the spot price.

11. If the expected spot price of soybean oil in one year is $3, determine the one-year futures price using discounted cash flow analysis. The T-bill rate is 8% and the market risk premium is 10%. The beta of soybean oil is -.65.

12. Given an 8% T-bill rate and a 10% market risk premium, calculate the one-year futures price for plywood. The beta of plywood is .66 and the expected spot price of plywood in one year is $8.

13. The T-bill rate is 8% and the market risk premium is 10%. Calculate the price of a one-year futures contract on oats if the beta of oats is 0 and the expected spot price in one year is $5.

14. You enter into an agreement to lend $462,963 now in exchange for $500,000 in one year. If the CPI is currently at 37.0, and the futures price is 380, what real rate of interest can you lock in through the use of CPI futures?

15. Answer Problem 14 assuming the CPI is currently at 360.

CFA PROBLEMS

16. (CFA Examination 1987, Level I) An investor who utilizes the U.S. Treasury bill futures market to hedge exchanges interest rate risk for:

    a. reinvestment risk
    b. credit risk
    c. basis risk
    d. sovereign risk

17. (CFA Examination 1986, Level I) Which statement regarding financial futures is not true?

    a. They normally are highly leveraged.
    b. They must be held until the expiration date.
    c. The market is very liquid.
    d. None of the above.

SOLUTIONS

1. $F_o = 280(1 + .04 - .02)$
   $= 285.6$

2. $F_o = 280(1 + .05 - .02)$
   $= 288.4$

3. $F_o = 280(1 + .04 - .04)$
   $= 280$

4. $F_o = 1.70(1.08/1.05)$
   $= 1.7486$

5. $F_o = 1.70(1.09/1.05)$
   $= 1.7648$

6. $F_o = 1.70(1.08/1.07)$
   $= 1.7159$

7.

Action	CF, t = 0	CF, t = 1
Borrow one pound in U.K., convert to dollars	1.70	$-E_1(1.05)$
Lend $1.70 in U.S.	-1.70	1.70 (1.08)
Go long in futures to purchase 1.05 pounds at $F_o = 1.72$		$1.05 (E_1 - 1.72)$
Total	0	.03

Make a profit of $.03 for every pound borrowed

8.
Action	CF, t = 0	CF, t = 1
Borrow $1.70 in U.S., convert to pounds	1.70	$-1.70\,(1.08)$
Lend one pound ($1.70) in U.K.	-1.70	$E_1\,(1.05)$
Go short in futures to deliver 1.05 pounds at $F_o = 1.76$		$1.05\,(1.76 - E_1)$
Total	0	.012

Make a profit of $.012 for every pound lent

9. $F_o = 600\,(1 + .08 + .01)$
$ = 654$

10. $F_o = 600\,(1 + .08 + .02)$
$ = 660$

11. Required rate of return $= .08 + -.65(.10) = .015$
$F_o = 3.00(1.08/1.015)$

$ = 3.19$

12. Required rate of return $= .08 + .66(.10) = .146$
$F_o = 8.00(1.08/1.146)$

$ = 7.54$

13. Required rate of return $= .08$
$F_o = 5.00(1.08/1.08)$

$ = 5.00$

14. If you go long 1.315789 futures, the payoff will be
1.315789 (CPI - 380) x 1000 = 1315.789 CPI - $500,000

When the futures position is combined with the loan repayment, the value of the portfolio is given by 1315.789 CPI, which is 131,578.9 real dollars. The $462,963 lent when the CPI is at 350 represents 125,125 real dollars. The real rate is given by

(131,578.9 - 125,125/125,125 = .0516

15. If the CPI is at 360, the $462,963 lent is 128,600.8 real dollars. The real rate is given by

(131,578.9 - 128,600.8)/128,600.8 = .0232

16. c
17. b

23 The Theory of Active Portfolio Management

OUTLINE

I. Active portfolio management in efficient markets

II. Objective of active portfolio management

III. Market timing

    A. The inadequacy of mean-variance analysis in valuing market timing

    B. Valuing market timing as an option

IV. The Treynor-Black model of security selection

    A. Model overview

    B. Construction of portfolios

V. Active portfolio management using multi-factor models

HIGHLIGHTS

Active portfolio management plays a central role in an efficient market. Without active management, the market would cease to be efficient. While it may not pay for a small investor to do the research to earn a small increase in return, it does pay for institutions that deal with multi-million dollar portfolios. The goal of active portfolio management is to construct a portfolio that maximizes the reward-to-variability ratio. Market timing is a simple form of active management, and the ability to time perfectly is shown to be equivalent to holding a call option on the market portfolio. The Treynor-Black model of security selection utilizes the single index model and a macroeconomic forecast to determine the normal expected returns on securities. These are compared to forecast returns, and the active portfolio is constructed by holding positive amounts of assets with positive expected abnormal returns and by shorting assets with negative expected abnormal returns. The weight of each asset in the active portfolio is proportional to the ratio of its abnormal return to its nonsystematic risk. The active portfolio is then combined with the market index to determine the optimal risky portfolio.

PROBLEMS

1. Calculate the Sharpe measure for the following funds. The T-bill rate was 8%.

Fund	Return	Standard Deviation
A	.14	.15
B	.16	.18
C	.18	.19

2. Which fund would be chosen by an investor with a risk-aversion coefficient A = 4, and what percentage of his wealth would be invested in the fund?

3. Answer Problem 2 for an investor with a risk-aversion coefficient A = 6.

4. Assume that market volatility is 6% per month and the T-bill rate

is 1% per month. What is the value of perfect market timing on a monthly basis?

5. Answer Problem 4 assuming market volatility is 7%.

6. Answer Problem 4 assuming the T-bill rate is 1.5% per month.

7. Using the information in Problem 4, what is the value of the following imperfect timers?

a. A: correctly predicted 12 of 20 months when the market did worse than T-bills and correctly predicted 32 of 40 months when the market return exceeded the T-bill rate.

b. B: correctly predicted 18 of 20 months when the T-bill rate exceeded the market returns and 22 of 40 months when the reverse was true.

Use the following information for Problems 8-13:

Macro Forecast

Asset	Expected Return	Standard Deviation
T-bills	.06	0
Passive equity portfolio	.16	.25

Micro Forecast

Stock	Expected Return	Beta	Residual Standard Deviation
A	.20	1.2	.56
B	.14	.9	.44
C	.22	1.3	.60

8. Calculate the alpha value for each of the stocks?

9. What is the weight of each asset in the active portfolio?

10. What is the Sharpe measure for the optimal risky portfolio?

11. Answer Problem 9 assuming short sales are not allowed.

12. Answer Problem 10 assuming short sales are not allowed.

SOLUTIONS

1. $S_A = (.14 - .08)/.15 = .4$

    $S_B = (.16 - .08)/.18 = .44$

    $S_C = (.18 - .08)/.19 = .53$

2. Fund C would be chosen by a risk-averse investor because it has the highest reward-to-variability ratio. The percentage of his wealth invested in the risky asset is given by

$$y = \frac{.18 - .08}{4(.0361)} = .69$$

3. Fund C would be chosen. The percentage of wealth invested in Fund C is given by

$$y = \frac{.18 - .08}{6(.0361)} = .46$$

4. Using Black/Scholes

   $X = S(1.01)$

   $$d_1 = \frac{\ln(1.01) + (.01 + .0036/2)}{.06} = .36$$

   $d_2 = .36 - .06 = .30$

   $N(d_1) = .6406$

   $N(d_2) = .6179$

   $C = S(.6406) - S(.6179) = .0227S$

5. $$d_1 = \frac{\ln(1.01) + (.01 + .0049/2)}{.07} = .32$$

   $d_2 = .32 - .07 = .25$

   $N(d_1) = .6255$

   $N(d_2) = .5987$

   $C = S(.6255) - S(.5987) = .0268S$

6. $$d_1 = \frac{\ln(1.05) + (.015 + .0036/2)}{.06} = 1.09$$

   $d_2 = 1.09 - .06 = 1.03$

   $N(d_1) = .8621$

   $N(d_2) = .8485$

   $C = S(.8621) - S(.8485) = .01365$

7. a. $P_1 = 12/20 = .6$

      $P_2 = 32/40 = .8$

Timing score = .6 + .8 − 1 = .4

Value = .4(.0227S) = .00908S

b. P_1 = 18/20 = .9

P_2 = 22/40 = .55

Timing score = .9 + .55 − 1 = .45

Value = .45(.0227S) = .010215S

8. The required rates of return from the SML

R_A = .06 + 1.2(.10) = .18

R_B = .06 + .9(.10) = .15

R_C = .06 + 1.3(.10) = .19

$alpha_A$ = .20 − .18 = .02

$alpha_B$ = .14 − .15 = −.01

$alpha_C$ = .22 − .19 = .03

9. $alpha_A/var(e_A)$ = $.02/.56^2$ = .06378

$alpha_B/var(e_B)$ = − $.01/.44^2$ = −.05165

$alpha_C/var(e_C)$ = $.03/.6^2$ = $\underline{.08333}$

total .09546

w_A = .06378/.09546 = .668

w_B = −.05165/.09546 = −.541

w_C = .08333/.09546 = $\underline{.873}$

1

10. $alpha_{active}$ = .668(.02) + (−.541)(−.01) + .873(.03) = .045

$$\beta_{active} = .668(1.2) + (-.541)(.9) + .873(1.3) = 1.45$$

$$var(e_{active}) = .668^2(.56^2) + (-.541^2)(.44^2) + .873^2(.6^2)$$

$$= .140 + .057 + .274$$

$$= .471$$

$$w_o = (.045/.471)/(.10/.25^2) = .06$$

$$w^* = \frac{.06}{1 + (1 - 1.45).06} = .062$$

$$S_p^2 = [(.16 - .06)/.25]^2 + [.045/(.471)^{.5}]^2$$

$$= .16 + .004$$

$$= .164$$

$S_p = .405$ compared to .40 for the passive portfolio.

11. Without short sales, only asset A will be in the active portfolio.

$$\alpha_A/var(e_A) = .06378$$

$$\alpha_C/var(e_C) = \underline{.08333} \quad .14711$$

$$w_A = .06378/.14711 = .434$$

$$w_C = .08333/.14711 = \underline{.566} \quad 1$$

12. $$\alpha_{active} = .434(.02) + .566(.03) = .026$$

$$\beta_{active} = .434(1.2) + .566(1.3) = 1.257$$

$$var(e_{active}) = .434^2(.56^2) + .566^2(.6^2)$$

$$= .059 + .115$$

$$= .174$$

$$w_o = (.026/.174)/(.10/.25^2) = .093$$

$$w^* = \frac{.093}{1 + (1 - 1.257)(.093)} = .095$$

$$S_p^2 = [(.16 - .06)/.25]^2 + [.045/(.174)^{.5}]^2$$

$$= .16 + .012$$

$$= .172$$

$$S_p = .415$$

24 Portfolio Performance Evaluation

OUTLINE

I. Measuring investment returns

    A. Time-weighted vs. dollar-weighted returns

    B. Arithmetic vs. geometric averages

II. The conventional theory of performance evaluation

    A. Procedure

    B. Measures

        1. Sharpe
        2. Treynor
        3. Jensen
        4. Appraisal ratio

    C. The selection of the proper measures

        1. The portfolio is the entire risky investment.
        2. The portfolio is mixed with the passive portfolio.
        3. The portfolio is part of a large, actively managed fund.

    D. An example of portfolio performance measurement

    E. Realized U.S. expected returns

III. The relationships among various performance measures

IV. Measuring performance with changing portfolio composition

V. Market timing

VI. Performance attribution

    1. Market allocation
    2. Sector selection
    3. Security selection

VII. Evaluating performance evaluation

HIGHLIGHTS

Evaluation of portfolio performance is complicated by the existence of alternative methods of calculating returns and averages. In addition, the choice of which performance measure to use depends on the role of the portfolio being evaluated. The Sharpe measure is appropriate when the portfolio is the entire investment fund, while the Treynor measure is appropriate for the portfolios that constitute the larger fund. The appraisal ratio is used when the portfolio will be mixed with a passive portfolio. Portfolio returns are "noisy," so that a large number of observations on returns is desirable in the evaluation process. This may not be possible due to a changing portfolio composition, with a resulting change in mean and variance. Performance can be partioned into the selection of markets, the selection of industries within each market, and the selection of securities within each industry. Despite the variety of performance measures, evaluation of portfolio performance is inadequate because data concerning the composition of portfolios is available only on a quarterly basis.

PROBLEMS

1. Consider the stock below that pays dividends of $2/share each year. Calculate the dollar-weighted return to an investor who purchases one share at t = 0, two shares at t = 1, and three shares at t = 2, and sells all the shares at t = 3.

Time	Stock Price
0	40
1	45
2	47
3	48

2. What is the time-weighted return to the investor in Problem 1?

3. Answer Problem 1 assuming the investor reverses his purchasing pattern: he buys three shares at t = 0, two shares at t = 1, and one share at t = 2.

4. Answer Problem 1 assuming the investor purchases one share at T=0, two shares at t = 1, and 100 shares at t = 2.

5. Calculate the geometric and arithmetic averages of returns for the stock below.

Year	Return
1	-.10
2	.30
3	.05
4	.15

6. Calculate the geometric and arithmetic averages of returns for the stock below.

Year	Return
1	-.30
2	.50
3	-.05
4	.25

Use the following information for Problems 7-11:

Below are the excess-return regression results for three portfolios. The risk free rate over the period was .07 and the market's average return was .15, and the standard deviation was .3.

Portfolio	Alpha	Beta	Standard Deviation	Residual Standard Deviation
A	.01	.8	.35	.20
B	.03	1.4	.55	.35
C	.02	1.2	.45	.25

7. Which portfolio is best using Jensen's measure?

8. Which portfolio is best using the Sharpe measure?

9. Which portfolio is best using the Treynor measure?

10. Which portfolio is best using the appraisal ratio?

11. Which portfolio would you hold if it is your only risky investment?

12. Given the following information, what was the underperformance or overperformance of the fund manager?

Market	Actual Return	Actual Weight	Benchmark Weight	Idex Return
Equity	.032	.50	.60	.03
Bonds	.013	.40	.30	.015
Cash	.01	.10	.10	.01

13. Decompose the performance in Problem 12 into the allocation and selection components.

14. Given the following information, what was the underperformance or overperformance of the manager?

Market	Actual Return	Actual Weight	Benchmark Weight	Index Return
Equity	.027	.70	.60	.024
Bonds	.018	.20	.30	.015
Cash	.005	.10	.10	.005

15. Decompose the performance in Problem 14 into the allocation and selection components.

CFA PROBLEMS

16. (CFA Examination 1986, Level I) A geometric average of a series of returns that range from -10% to +25% is less than an arithmetic average of those same returns:

    a. only when both averages are positive.
    b. only when both averages are negative.
    c. only when the standard deviation of returns is higher than the arithmetic average of the returns.
    d. under all circumstances.

17. (CFA Examination 1986, Level I) The spread between an arithmetic average and a geometric average:

    a. increases as the variability of the returns increases.
    b. increases as the variability of the returns decreases.
    c. is always zero.
    d. depends on the specific returns being averaged, but is not necessarily sensitive to their variability.

18. (CFA Examination 1986, Level I) The time-weighted rate of return as a measure of a portfolio manager's performance is

    a. more appropriate than the internal rate of return because it accounts for cash flows to and from the portfolio.
    b. inappropriate because it is affected by the timing and size of contributions to the portfolio.
    c. affected by disbursements from the portfolio, but is not affected by contributions to the portfolio.
    d. always identical to the internal rate of return of the portfolio.

SOLUTIONS

1. The dollar-weighted return is the value of k that solves the following:

   $$40 + 90/(1 + k) + 141/(1 + k)^2 =$$
   $$2/(1 + k) + 6/(1 + k)^2 + 300/(1 + k)^3$$
   $$k = .0825$$

2. The time-weighted return is the average of three time period returns.

   $r_1 = (45 - 40 + 2)/40 = .175$

   $r_2 = (47 - 45 + 2)/45 = .0889$

   $r_3 = (48 - 47 + 2)/47 = .0638$

   Time-weighted return = $(.175 + .0889 + .0638)/3 = .1092$

3. The dollar weighted return is the value of k that solves the following:

   $$120 + 90/(1 + k) + 47/(1 + k)^2 =$$
   $$6/(1 + k) + 10/(1 + k)^2 + 300/(1 + k)^3$$
   $$k = .0969$$

4. The dollar-weighted return is the value of k that solves the following:

   $$40 + 90/(1 + k) + 4700/(1 + k)^2 =$$
   $$2/(1 + k) + 6/(1 + k)^2 + 5150/(1 + k)^3$$
   $$k = .0696$$

5. Geometric average

   $r = [(.9)(1.3)(1.05)(1.15)]^{.25} - 1 = .0902$

   Arithmetic average

   $r = (-.10 + .30 + .05 + .15)/4 = .10$

6. Geometric average

   $r = [(.7)(1.5)(.95)(1.25)]^{.25} - 1 = .0567$

   Arithmetic average

$r = (-.3 + .5 + -.05 + .25)/4 = .10$

7. Jensen's measure is just the alpha from the regression, so portfolio C is the best.

8. Average return$_A$ = .07 + .8(.08) + .01 = .144

   Average return$_B$ = .07 + 1.4(.08) + .03 = .212

   Average return$_C$ = .07 + 1.2(.08) + .02 = .186

   $S_A = (.144 - .07)/.35 = .2114$

   $S_B = (.212 - .07)/.55 = .2582$

   $S_C = (.186 - .07)/.45 = .2577$

   Portfolio B is best using the Sharpe measure.

9. $T_A = (.144 - .07)/.8 = .0925$

   $T_B = (.212 - .07)/1.4 = .1014$

   $T_C = (.186 - .07)/1.2 = .0967$

   Portfolio B is best using the Treynor measure.

10. A: .01/.20 = .05
    B: .03/.35 = .0857
    C: .02/.25 = .08

    Portfolio B is best using the appraisal ratio.

11. You would choose the market portfolio, a passive strategy, as it has a Sharpe measure of

    $(.15 - .07)/.3 = .2667$

12. Return on portfolio = .5(.032) + .4(.013) + .1(.01) = .0222

    Return on benchmark portfolio = .6(.03) + .3(.015) + .1(.01) = .0235

    The fund manager underperformed by 13 basis points.

    Contribution of selection to total performance:

Market	Excess Performance	Portfolio Weight	Contribution
Equity	.003	.7	.0021
Bonds	.003	.2	.0006
			.0027

Selection contributed 27 of the 36 basis points of overperformance.

13. Contribution of asset allocation to performance.

Market	Excess Weight	Index Return	Contribution
Equity	−.10	.03	−.003
Bonds	.10	.015	.0015
Cash	0	.01	0
			−.0015

The fund manager lost 15 basis points for poor allocation.

Contribution of selection to total performance

market	excess performance	portfolio weight	contribution
equity	.002	.5	.0010
bonds	−.002	.4	−.0008
			.0002

Selection netted to two basis points. The manager was good at choosing equities and bad at selecting bonds.

14. Return on portfolio = .7(.027) + .2(.018) + .1(.005) = .023

Return on benchmark portfolio = .6(.024) + .3(.015) + .1(.005) = .0194

The fund manager overperformed by 36 basis points.

15. Contribution of asset allocation to performance:

Market	Excess Weight	Index Return	Contribution
Equity	.1	.024	.0024
Bonds	−.1	.015	−.0015
Cash	0	.005	0
			.0009

The manager netted to gaining nine basis points for allocation.

16. d

17. a

18. a

25 International and Extended Diversification

OUTLINE

I. International investments

    A. The world market portfolio

    B. International diversification

II. Exchange rate risk

III. International investing

    A. Passive vs. active investing

    B. Factor models

IV. Equilibrium in international markets

V. Other investments

    A. Real estate

    B. Metals

HIGHLIGHTS

An investor who wishes to maximize the benefits of diversification will look beyond stocks and bonds. Foreign securities offer excellent diversification possibilities because of the lower correlation of their returns with the returns on U.S. securities. There is a risk in foreign investment, however, that is not present in domestic investment. This is exchange rate risk, which arises because the investor will have to convert the proceeds of the foreign investment into dollars at some uncertain exchange rate. This risk may be hedged by use of the forward and futures markets in currencies. Factor analysis indicates that an international factor is important in pricing assets. Diversification is also possible through real estate and metals, and both have been shown to be excellent inflation hedges.

PROBLEMS

Use the following information for Problems 1-8:

You plan to invest $100,000 for one year in a British stock that is selling for $50 pounds/share. The current exchange rate is $2/pound. At the end of the year the price per share will be either 60 pounds, 50 pounds, or 40 pounds and the exchange rate will be either $1.70/pound, $2.0/pound or $2.30/pound.

1. How many shares can you purchase?

2. What is the pound-denominated return in each state?

3. What is the dollar-denominated return in each state?

4. Assuming each state is equally probable, what is the standard deviation of the pound-denominated return?

5. Assuming each state is equally probable, what is the standard deviation of the dollar-denominated return?

6. How many pounds should be sold forward to hedge this risk?

7. If the current exchange rate is $1.80/pound, the one-year forward rate is $2.0/pound, and the British risk-free rate is 9%, what is the dollar-denominated risk-free rate that can be obtained by investing in the British risk-free asset?

8. Answer Problem 7 assuming the current exchange rate is $1.60/pound.

Use the following information for Problems 9-12:

Market	EAFE Weight	Return on Equity Index	E_1/E_0	Manager's Weight	Manager's Return
Europe	.30	.22	.95	.30	.24
Australia	.10	.16	1.10	.20	.18
Far East	.60	.26	1.20	.50	.24

9. Did this manager underperform or overperform?

10. What part of the performance is due to currency selection?

11. What part of the performance is due to country selection?

12. What part of the performance is due to stock selection?

Use the following information for Problems 13-16:

Market	EAFE Weight	Return on Equity Index	E_1/E_0	Manager's Weight	Manager's Return
Europe	.30	.20	.9	.40	.22
Australia	.10	.15	1.2	.30	.18
Far East	.60	.35	1.3	.30	.35

13. Did the manager underperform or overperform?

14. What part of the performance is due to currency selection?

15. What part of the performance is due to country selection?

16. What part of the performance is due to stock selection?

CFA PROBLEMS

17. (CFA Examination 1985, Level I) List three factors that affect relative foreign exchange rates.

18. (CFA Examination 1987, Level I) Unique risks are associated with international investing. Briefly describe three such risks.

19. (CFA Examination 1986, Level I) A primary reason for an investor to buy international bonds is that these bonds have:

   a. less exposure to currency fluctuations than domestic bonds
   b. low correlation of returns with domestic bonds
   c. superior rates of return compared to domestic bonds
   d. less interest rate risk than domestic bonds

SOLUTIONS

1. 100,000/2 = 50,000 pounds   50,000/50 = 1000 shares

2. $P_1 = 40$, return = (40 - 50)/50 = -.20

   $P_1 = 50$, return = 0

   $P_1 = 60$, return = (60 - 50)/50 = .20

3. The dollar value of 1,000 shares at year end is given below.

Year-End Exchange Rate

Price	$1.70	$2.00	$2.30
40	40x1000x1.7 = $68,000	40x1000x2 = $80,000	40x1000x2.3 = $ 92,000
50	50x1000x1.7 = $85,000	50x1000x2 = $100,000	50x1000x2.3 = $115,000
60	60x1000x1.7 = $102,000	60x1000x2 = $120,000	60x1000x2.3 = $138,000

Starting with $100,000 the returns are

Year-End Exchange Rate

Price	$1.70	$2.00	$2.30
40	-.32	-.20	-.08
50	-.15	0	.15
60	.02	.20	.38

4. Expected return = 0

   $\text{Var} = 1/3(-.2 - 0)^2 + 1/3(0) + 1/3(.2 - 0)^2$
   $= .026667$
   Std dev = .163

5. Expected return = $(-.32 - .15 + .02 - .2 + 0 + .2 - .08 + .15 + .38)/9 = 0$

   $\text{Var} = [(-.32)^2 + (-.15)^2 + .02^2 + (-.2)^2 + 0 + .2^2 + (-.08)^2 + .15^2 + .38^2]/9$

   $= [.1024 + .0225 + .0004 + .04 + 0 + .04 + .0064 + .0225 + .1444]/9$
   $= .0421$
   std dev = .205

6. 50,000

7. To illustrate, assume an investment of $18,000.

   t = 0, exchange $18,000 for 10,000 pounds
   t = 0, sell forward 10,900 pounds at $2/pound
   t = 1, exchange 10,900 pounds for $21,800
       Return = ($21,800 - $18,000)/$18,000
          = .211

8. Assume $16,000 to invest

   t = 0, exchange $16,000 for 10,000 pounds
   t = 0, sell forward 10,900 pounds at $2/pound
   t = 1, exchange 10,900 pounds for $21,800
       Return = ($21,800 - $16,000)/$16,000
          = .3625

9. Actual return = .3(.24) + .2(.18) + .5(.24) = .228
    EAFE   = .3(.22) + .1(.16) + .6(.26) = .238
    The manager underperformed by 100 basis points.

10. Currency selection
    Manager   .3(.95) + .2(1.1) + .5(1.2) = 1.105
    EAFE   .3(.95) + .1(1.1) + .6(1.2) = 1.115
    Loss of 10% compared to relative to EAFE.

11. Country selection
    Manager   .3(.22) + .2(.16) + .5(.26) = .228
    EAFE   .3(.22) + .1(.16) + .6(.26) = .238
    Loss of 100 basis points relative to EAFE.

12. Stock selection
    .3(.24 - .22) + .2(.18 - .16) + .5(.24 - .26) = 0

13. Actual return = .4(.22) + .3(.18) + .3(.35) = .247
    EAFE   = .3(.20) + .1(.15) + .6(.35) = .285
    The manager underperformed by 380 basis points.

14. Currency selection
    Manager   .4(.9) + .3(1.2) + .3(1.3) = 1.11
    EAFE   .3(.9) + .1(1.2) + .6(1.3) = 1.17
    Loss of 6% relative to EAFE.

15. Country selection
    Manager   .4(.20) + .3(.15) + .3(.35) = .23
    EAFE   .3(.20) + .1(.15) + .6(.35) = .285
    Loss of 550 basis points relative to EAFE.

16. Stock selection
    .4(.22 - .20) + .3(.18 - .15) + .3(0) = .017
    Gained 170 basis points relative to EAFE.

17. Select three of the following factors:

    a. The balance of payments and prospective changes in that balance

    b. The inflation rate and the outlook for inflation

    c. Interest rate differentials between countries

    d. The social and political atmosphere, particularly with regard to the impact on foreign investment

    e. Central bank intervention in the currency markets

18. Four primary risks are:

a. **Currency fluctuations**. If the value of the investor's domestic currency strengthens after the purchase of foreign securities, the value of the investment declines.

b. **Availability of information**. Quality information about foreign companies may be less readily available to analysts than information about domestic companies. This is because of varying requirements for corporate disclosure, less exhaustive analysis conducted by the foreign financial community, and the use of accounting conventions that differ from those in the country of the investor.

c. **Liquidity**. Foreign equity issues may tend to be smaller (or larger) than those in the investor's country, making the accumulation of substantial positions more (or less) difficult.

d. **Sovereign risks**. These risks include the potential for disruptive political, sociological, or psychological developments. Examples of political risk are the possibility of nationalization of local companies, expropriation of assets owned by foreign investors, punitive taxation, and restrictions on the withdrawal of capital.

Other unique risks that might be addressed are:

e. High transaction costs, including taxes

f. Administrative cost/settlement problems

g. High fee structure and difficulty in assessing manager skill.

19. b

26 Organizational Structure and Management Issues

OUTLINE

I. The organization of a portfolio management firm

    A. The Index Portfolio Group

        1. Macro forecasting
        2. Using macro forecasts
        3. Objectives and management of the index portfolio

    B. The Active Portfolio Group

        1. Micro forecasting
        2. Adjustments to micro forecasts
        3. Managing security analysts
        4. Optimizing the active portfolio

    C. The Safe Asset Group

        1. Incurring interest rate risk
        2. Incurring default risk

    D. The Complete Portfolio Group

        1. Optimizing the complete portfolio
        2. Managing the Complete Portfolio Group

    E. The Data, Resources, and Estimation Group

        1. Data bases
        2. Estimation
        3. Optimization

    F. The Evaluation and Attribution Group

        1. Principles of evaluation
        2. Evaluation of the individual forecaster

    G. The Cleaning and Transaction Unit

II. Logistics

III. Accounting and financial control

IV. Marketing and sales

V. Personnel and physical plant

HIGHLIGHTS

An efficient investment management firm may take the form described in the chapter. The complete portfolio is formed from three other portfolios, each actively managed. The Index Portfolio Group, using macro forecasts and beta forecasts, attempts to construct an efficient index-like portfolio. The Active Portfolio Group attempts to discover mispriced securities and form a portfolio of these using the Treynor-Black model. The Safe Asset Group attempts to improve on the yield offered by T-bills by incurring small amounts of interest rate risk and/or default risk. The Data, Resources, and Estimation Group provides forecasts and data to the other groups, while the Evaluation and Attribution Group provides performance evaluation.

PROBLEMS

1. The raw macro forecast for one-year excess market return is .16. The long-run average excess return on the market has been .09. Using the information below on past macro forecasts, calculate the adjusted macro forecast.

Year	-1	-2	-3	-4	-5	-6
Forecast excess return	.24	.24	.20	-.05	-.15	0
Actual excess return	.20	.28	.26	-.10	-.05	-.05

2. Answer Problem 1 assuming the macro forecast for excess market return was .11.

3. Given the information below on past forecasts of excess market return, calculate the adjusted forecast. The raw forecast of excess market return is .14, and the long-run average of excess market return has been .08.

Year	-1	-2	-3	-4	-5	-6
Forecast excess return	.23	.25	.18	-.20	-.20	.16
Actual excess return	.15	.20	.23	-.25	-.05	.20

4. Answer Problem 3 assuming the macro forecast for excess market return was .10.

Use the following information for Problems 5-11:

A share of ABC stock is currently selling for $20. An analyst covering the stock thinks the fair end-of-quarter price for the stock is $22.50. The stock has a beta of 1.8, the 90-day T-bill rate is .015, and the adjusted macro forecast is for a market rate

of return of .04 over the next quarter. The analyst's record of
similar predictions is given below. The stock pays no dividends

Market Price	Forecast End-of-Period Price	Actual End of Period Price	Market Forecast	Actual Market Return	T-Bill Rate
$12.00	$14.00	$13.00	.05	.10	.015
$18.00	$21.50	$15.00	.04	.10	.02
$16.00	$17.50	$14.50	.02	-.05	.015
$13.50	$13.00	$12.00	-.01	-.03	.015

5. What is the unadjusted forecast of alpha, S, from the analyst?

6. Calculate the past expected returns obtained from the analyst's forecasts of price.

7. Calculate the past expected returns obtained from the single index model, using the market forecast.

8. What were the past actual returns on the stock?

9. What were the past returns expected from the actual SML?

10. What are the past forecast alphas, and what are the past actual alphas?

11. What is the adjusted forecast of alpha?

12. If the residual standard deviation of the stock is estimated at .30, what is the ability-adjusted estimate?

SOLUTIONS

1. The adjusted forecast is obtained by multiplying the difference between the raw forecast and the long-run mean by the square of the correlation coefficient between forecast and actual values.

$\text{Mean}_{actual} = (.20 + .28 + .26 - .10 - .05 - .05)/6 = .09$

$\text{Mean}_{forecast} = (.24 + .24 + .20 - .05 - .15 + 0)/6 = .08$

$\text{Var}_{actual} = [(.20 - .09)^2 + (.28 - .09)^2 + (.26 - .09)^2 + (-.10 - .09)^2 + (-.05 - .09)^2 + (-.05 - .09)^2]/6$

$\phantom{\text{Var}_{actual}} = (.0121 + .0361 + .0289 + .0361 + .0196 + .0196)/6$
$\phantom{\text{Var}_{actual}} = .0254$
$\text{Std dev} = .15937$

$\text{Var}_{forecast} = [(.24 - .08)^2 + (.24 - .08)^2 + (.20 - .08)^2 + (-.05 - .08)^2 + (-.15 - .08)^2 + (0 - .08)^2]/6$

$\phantom{\text{Var}_{forecast}} = (.0256 + .0256 + .0144 + .0169 + .0529 + .0064)/6$
$\phantom{\text{Var}_{forecast}} = .02363$
$\text{Std dev} = .15373$

$\text{Cov} = [.11(.16) + .19(.16) + .17(.12) + (-.19)(-.13) + (-.14)(-.23) + (-.14)(-.08)]/6$

$\phantom{\text{Cov}} = (.0176 + .0304 + .0204 + .0247 + .0322 + .0112)/6$
$\phantom{\text{Cov}} = .02275$

$\text{Corr} = \dfrac{.02275}{.15937(.15373)} = .92857$

Ability parameter $= .92857^2 = .862$

Adjusted macro forecast $= .09 + .862(.07) = .15034$

2. Adjusted macro forecast = .09 + .862(.02) = .10724

3. Mean_{actual} = (.15 + .20 + .23 − .25 − .05 + .20)/6 = .08

   $\text{Mean}_{forecast}$ = (.23 + .25 + .18 − .20 − .20 + .16)/6 = .07

   Var_{actual} = $[(.15 - .08)^2 + (.20 - .08)^2 + (.23 - .08)^2$
   $+ (-.25 - .08)^2 + (-.05 - .08)^2 + (.20 - .08)^2]/6$

   = (.0049 + .0144 + .0225 + .1089 + .0169 + .0144)/6
   = .03033

   Std dev = .17416

   $\text{Var}_{forecast}$ = $[(.23 - .07)^2 + (.25 - .07)^2 + (.18 - .07)^2$
   $+ (-.20 - .07)^2 + (-.20 - .07)^2 + (.16 - .07)^2]/6$

   = (.0256 + .0324 + .0121 + .0729 + .0729 + .0081)/6
   = .03733

   Std dev = .19322

   Cov = [.07(.16) + .12(.18) + .15(.11) + (−.33)(−.27)
   + (−.13)(−.27) + .12(.09)]/6

   = (.0112 + .0216 + .0165 + .0891 + .0351 + .0108)/6
   = .03072

   Corr = $\frac{.03072}{(.17416)(.19322)}$ = .91289

   Ability parameter = $.91289^2$ = .833

   Adjusted macro forecast = .08 + .833(.06) = .12998

4. Adjusted macro forecast = .08 + .833(.02) = .09666

5. The analyst expects a return of (22.50 − 20)/20 = .125.

   From the SML, the expected return is

   .015 + 1.8(.04) = .087

   Alpha = .125 − .087 = .038

6. a. (14.00 − 12.00)/12.00 = .1667

   b. (21.50 − 18.00)/18.00 = .1944

   c. (17.50 − 16.00)/16.00 = .0938

   d. (13.00 − 13.50)/13.50 = −.0370

7. a. .015 + 1.8(.05) = .105

    b.   .02 + 1.8(.04) = .092

    c.   .015 + 1.8(.02) = .051

    d.   .015 + 1.8(-.01) = -.003

8. a.   (13.00 - 12.00)/12.00 = .0833

    b.   (15.00 - 18.00)/18.00 = -.1667

    c.   (14.50 - 16.00)/16.00 = -.0938

    d.   (12.00 - 13.50)/13.50 = -.1111

9. a.   .015 + 1.8(.10) = .195

    b.   .02 + 1.8(.10) = .20

    c.   .015 + 1.8(-.05) = -.075

    d.   .015 + 1.8(-.03) = -.039

10. Forecast alphas

    a.   .1667 - .105 = .0617

    b.   .1944 - .092 = .1024

    c.   .0938 - .051 = .0428

    d.   -.0370 - (-.003) = -.034

    Actual alphas

    a.   .0833 - .195 = -.1117

    b.   -.1667 - .20 = -.3667

    c.   -.0938 - (-.075) = -.0188

    d.   -.1111 - (-.039) = -.0721

11. $\text{Mean}_{\text{forecast}} = (.0617 + .1024 + .0428 - .034)/4 = .0432$

    $\text{Mean}_{\text{actual}} = (-.1117 - .3667 - .0188 - .0721)/4 = -.1423$

    $\text{Var}_{\text{forecast}} = [(.0617 - .0432)^2 + (.1024 - .0432)^2$
                      $+ (.0428 - .0432)^2 - (-.034 - .0432)^2]/4$

                 = (.00034225 + .00350464 + .00000016 + .00595984)/4
                 = .00245

    Std dev = .04951

$$\text{Var}_{\text{actual}} = [(-.1117 + .1423)^2 + (-.3667 + .1423)^2 \\ + (-.0188 + .1423)^2 + (-.072 + .1423)^2]/4$$

$$= (.00093636 + .05035536 + .01525225 + .00494209)/4$$
$$= .017871515$$
$$\text{Std dev} = .13368$$

$$\text{Cov} = [.0185(.0306) + .0592(-.2244) + (-.0004)(.1235) \\ + (-.0772)(-.0703)]/4$$
$$= (.0005661 - .01328448 - .0000494 - .00542716)/4$$
$$= .004548735$$

$$\text{Corr} = \frac{.000385}{(.04951)(.13368)} = -.687$$

Ability parameter $= -.687^2 = .472$

Adjusted alpha $= .087(.472) = .041064$

12. Adjusted standard deviation $= (1 - .472).30 = .1584$

27 Principles of Portfolio Management

OUTLINE

I. Objectives
    A. Return requirements
    B. Risk tolerance

II. Types of investors
    A. Individuals
    B. Personal trusts
    C. Mutual funds
    D. Pension funds
    E. Endowment funds
    F. Life insurance companies
    G. Nonlife insurance companies
    H. Banks

III. Constraints
    A. Liquidity
    B. Time horizon
    C. Legal and regulatory
    D. Tax status

IV. Asset allocation
    A. Specification of included asset classes
    B. Specification of capital market expectations

C. Deviation of the efficient frontier

D. Determination of the optimal asset mix

E. Diversification into other asset classes

F. Hedging against inflation

G. Taxes and asset allocation

HIGHLIGHTS

The chapter distinguishes among seven classes of investors who in general have different investment objectives, different constraints, and different portfolio policies. For each investor, the asset allocation process consists of specifying which types of assets are to be included in the portfolio, specifying the expectations with regard to the capital market, determining the efficient frontier, and determining the optimal asset mix. For investors who must pay taxes on certain types of investment income, the situation is more complicated. The principle of avoiding taxes may conflict with the principle of efficient diversification.

CFA PROBLEMS

1. (CFA Examination 1983, Level I) Describe briefly the key elements in the decision making process for the management of investment portfolios.

2. (CFA Examination 1987, Level I) Jack Quick and Heidi Bronson have been discussing the CFA Level I study materials as they relate to the determination of portfolio policies for different types of investors. Quick remembers reading that behind all investment portfolios are investors, each of whom is unique, and that there is literally a different set of portfolio management opportunities, needs, and circumstances for every investor. Because of this diversity of investor situations, Quick has concluded that it is impossible to generalize about portfolio policy determination - everything must be done on a case-by-case basis. Bronson agrees in terms of specific portfolio construction but reminds Quick that there is a framework illustrated in the readings through which portfolio policies can be established for even the broadest range of investor types and interests.

   a. Outline a broadly applicable framework for establishing portfolio policies, incorporating objectives and constraints, such as the one that Bronson has recalled.

   b. Bronson is working on a defined benefit retirement portfolio for a sizable and growing corporation with a young work force. Quick is working on a modest personal portfolio now providing essential income to a 70-year-old widow whose assets pass on her death to her children. Apply your Part a framework to each of the above investment situations, taking into account all of the relevant framework elements. (You may find it helpful to use a matrix format for this answer.)

3. (CFA Examination 1982, Level I) C. B. Snow, recently deceased president of Highway Cartage Company, left a net estate of $300,000. Under his will, a trust of $300,000 was created for his surviving spouse, with Peninsular Trust Company named trustee. A daughter is the remainderman of her mother's trust. The widow's trust is comprised of the following assets:

	Amount at Market	Current Yield
Money market fund	$ 75,000	14.7%
Tax-exempt municipal bonds	105,000	8.0(a)
Highway Cartage Co. Common stock	120,000	7.9
	$300,000	

(a) Yield to maturity equals 12.0%.

As a portfolio manager with Peninsular, you have just attended a meeting with the widow and learned the following:

- She is 65 and in good health (mortality tables indicate an expected life span of 18 years). As a retirement benefit, she is eligible for Highway's generous group medical insurance plan for the remainder of her life.

- Her estimated household and other expenses last year, adjusted to allow for inflation this year, indicate a need for at least $28,000 in pretax income. In the absence of her husband's salary, her tax bracket will decline substantially to 30%.

- Next week she will be eligible to receive Social Security payments of $600 per month.

- She plans to purchase a $60,000 condominium as a vacation residence within the next six months, using $15,000 in deferred compensation (after taxes) due her husband as the down payment. Conventional mortgage financing is available for 75% of the cost at 17.5% for 30 years. She anticipates that any tax savings from the credit for mortgage interest payments will be consumed by maintenance fees charged to condominium owners. She also intends to join an adjacent golf club where dues are $125 per month.

- She wishes to retain all of the Highway common stock because "It's the only stock C. B. ever owned and he had such great confidence in the company's future. Also, the yield is very generous, I think, despite the dividend reduction last year when the economy sagged."

At the conclusion of the meeting, Mrs. Snow requested that the assets in her trust be left intact if possible. Mrs. Snow is co-trustee of her trust and can veto any of your recommendations.

a. Calculate Mrs. Snow's income sources and expenses assuming her request is honored, and state whether her income requirements can be met.

b. Identify and discuss the investment objectives and constraints which appear applicable to Mrs. Snow's situation.

c. Recommend and justify changes in her present trust portfolio which are consistent with the objectives and constraints in Part b.

EXHIBIT I

MARKET DATA

Fixed Income Securities

Category	Current Market Yield
Money Market Funds	14.7%
Government Bonds:	
Intermediate-Term	14.4
Long-Term	14.0
Corporate Bonds (A-Rated):	
Intermediate-Term	15.1
Long-Term	16.0
Tax-Exempt Municipals:	
Intermediate-Term	10.2
Long-Term	11.1

Common Stocks

Category	Current Yield	Implied Total Return	Beta Coefficient
Industrials	5.2%	17.0%	1.0
Trucking	4.0	14.8	1.1
Highway Cartage Co.	7.9	14.8	1.3

Consumer Price Index

(Avg. Annual Increase)

Current Year	Next Year	Projected Next Five Years	
		Range	Most Probable
8.9%	8.0%	5-15%	7-10%

SOLUTIONS

1. The decision-making process can be outlined as follows:

    Specification and qualification of investor objectives, constraints, and preferences in the form of an investment policy statement.

    Determination and quantification of capital market expectations for the economy, market sectors, industries, and individual securities.

    Performance measurement and evaluation to ensure attainment of the investor objectives.

    Monitoring the portfolio factors and responding to changes in investor objectives and constraints and/or capital market expectations.

    Rebalancing the portfolio when necessary by repeating the asset allocation, portfolio strategy, security selection, and implementation steps.

2. a. Stated below is a broadly applicable framework for establishing investment policies, in which investor objectives are expressed in return/risk terms and constraints/preferences are stated in an appropriately specific manner. This framework is taken directly from the Maginn and Tuttle readings (Chapters 4 and 5).

    Investment Policy Framework Outline

    Objectives

    Return requirements
    Risk tolerance

    Constraints/Preferences

    Time horizon
    Liquidity requirements
    Tax considerations
    Legal/regulatory considerations
    Unique needs and circumstances

    Virtually any investment situation can be analyzed within the above framework to establish an investment policy and produce a management plan that is specific and appropriate to the particular investor situation involved. Details will differ in every case, but the framework itself will be applicable across the broad range of potential investor types and interests.

b.

Objectives	Pension Fund Portfolio	Widow's Personal Portfolio
Return requirements: Both need inflation protection but pension portfolio can take it in capital appreciation form whereas widow must get it in current income form	Total return-oriented; "income" needs low	"Income"-oriented; current needs high, and if income becomes insufficient she may have to sell some principal
Risk tolerance:	Above-average capacity and interim flexibility	Below-average capacity: "safety" primary consideration

Constraints/Preferences

	Pension Fund Portfolio	Widow's Personal Portfolio
Time Horizon:	Very long term: no known termination	Finite term; perhaps quite short for the widow
Liquidity requirements:	Probably low, and likely to remain so	Probably moderate now, but could become high at death
Tax considerations:	None, if a U.S. ERISA plan	Full personal income tax rates apply
Legal/regulatory considerations:	ERISA "Prudent Expert" rules; portfolio viewed as a whole	"Prudent man" rules if managed by advisor; portfolio assets viewed individually
Unique needs and circumstances:	None identified but cash inflows will continue and "deep pocket" available to cover shortfalls	Widow's income needs govern now, but children's interests and coming need for liquidity must be considered in planning. No "deep pocket" available.

3. a. Sources of Annualized Income are:

Trust assets:	
Money market fund ($75,000 x 14.7%)	$11,025
Tax exempt municipals ($105,000 x 8.0%)	8,400
Highway Cartage common ($120,000 x 7.9%)	9,480
	28,905
Social Security ($600 x 12)	7,200
	$36,105
Annualized expenses are:	
Household and other last year	$28,000
Mortgage on new second home ($45,000 x 17.5%)	7,875
Country club dues ($125 x 12)	1,500
	$37,375

    Income needs cannot be met by the existing portfolio ($37,375 - $36,100 = $1,270 shortfall).

    b. Investment objectives for Mrs. Snow should be defined in terms of the risk/return relationship.

    Return--To maintain her desired standard of living, the current income component of return must approximate 10% before taxes, a modest increase from the present level. Total return, including a capital change component, must be larger to assume maintenance of "real" income for an extended period (18 years) and preservation of as much principal as possible for the ultimate benefit of her daughter.

    Risk--Classified as being in the final phase of the "life cycle," Mrs. Snow should not risk permanent loss of principal by investment in risky categories of assets or assets having high nonsystematic risk. Since the trust must provide the majority (81%) of her living expenses, current income volatility must also be avoided. Because the corpus appears sufficient to meet current needs without downgrading quality or sacrificing diversification, market volatility can be tolerated.

    In summary, a realistic objective for Mrs. Snow is to increase return to at least 10% and maintain or decrease portfolio risk through improved diversification by asset category.

    Investment constraints to consider are:

    Liquidity--Needs are low since she has anticipated her largest discretionary capital and routine expenses. Moreover, the usual risk of large and unpredictable medical expenses for the elderly is not material because of full medical insurance coverage.

<u>Time horizon</u>--The time horizon is long enough to make inflation a significant risk factor. Therefore, attention to asset value preservation is important to the income beneficiary (Mrs. Snow) as well as the remainderman.

<u>Nondiversified equity portfolio</u>--The emotional request of Mrs. Snow to retain all Highway Cartage common and her veto power as co-trustee may limit portfolio construction options.

c. Recommended changes in Mrs. Snow's portfolio should include actions to improve diversification, increase current income, and reduce nonsystematic risk within the equity segment of the portfolio. Specifically, these would include:

Decrease liquidity (the money market fund) from 25% to 5% to 10% of assets because:

> Money market rates tend to fluctuate widely from year to year, which is in conflict with the assured minimum level of income objective.

> The inflation outlook in Exhibit I indicates the possibility for lower yields over the near and long term, which implies the possibility of an extended reduction in short-term yields.

Sell the tax-exempt municipal bonds (35% of assets) and purchase intermediate-term government and/or corporate bonds. In addition, add 5% to 15% of assets to this category with proceeds from the money market fund. The reasons are:

> After-tax income is increased and stabilized. Current yield is more important than yield to maturity since cash income is needed. Because of her change from a 60% to 30% tax bracket, taxable issues are more attractive on a net yield basis: (10.2% + (100% - 30%) = 14.6% taxable equivalent yield, which is less than 15.1% taxable yields available).

> Both near- and long-term projected inflation rates indicate a "real" rate of return is available from intermediate bonds.

> Principal volatility caused by interest rate fluctuations prior to maturity is not a major risk factor.

> Long-term bonds are not attractive because the incremental yield over intermediates is small and inflation remains a risk as per Exhibit I.

Sell the Highway Cartage common stock (40% of assets) and buy a diversified portfolio of industrial common stocks (40% to 50% of assets). The reasons are:

> The stock portfolio should be diversified rather than concentrated in one company in one industry.
>
> Highway's recent dividend cut suggests that elimination of the dividend is possible and that serious company and/or industry problems exist. The emotional request of Mrs. Snow must be evaluated in conjunction with Exhibit I, which indicates the risk-adjusted return of this issue is inferior to trucking company stocks and other industrial stocks. Highway is probably not appropriate even as a small percentage of the total portfolio.
>
> A diversified portfolio of industrial common stocks should provide superior returns over the long term relative to other investment options offered. While a "defensive," "late state" investor, Mrs. Snow needs inflation protection and assurance of a "real" return over many years. The reduction in current income yield from 7.9% to 5.2% will not jeopardize current income needs.

In summary, the following asset mix would satisfy Mrs. Snow's objectives:

	Amount	Percent of Portfolio	Current Yield	Annual Income
Money market fund	$ 30,000	10%	14.7%	$ 4,410
Government/corporate bonds (intermediate term)	$120,000-$150,000	40%-50%	14.5%	$19,575[a]
Common stocks	120,000-$150,000	40% 50%	5.2%	$7,020[a]
	$300,000	100%		$31,005

[a] Calculated on basis of midpoint of $135,000 each.

28 Individual Investors and Pension Funds

OUTLINE

I. The life cycle approach
   A. The consumption - retirement savings approach
   B. Human capital risk and insurance
   C. Home ownership as a hedge
   D. Buy vs. rent decision
   E. Asset allocation over the life cycle

II. Tax sheltering
   A. Tax deferral of capital gains
   B. Tax-deferred retirement plans
   C. Deferred annuities
   D. Variable and universal life insurance

III. Fallacies of conventional wisdom
   A. Risk in the long run
   B. Growth vs. income

IV. Pension plans
   A. Defined contribution plans
   B. Defined benefit plans
   C. The Black-Dewhurst proposal

HIGHLIGHTS

The life cycle approach to portfolio management views the individual as becoming more risk-averse as he ages due to the depletion of human capital and the decreased time to supply additional labor. Life and disability insurance serve to hedge the risk of lost human capital and future earning power. Besides investing in tax-exempt bonds, the investor can shelter income from taxes through investing in assets whose return comes in price appreciation, by investing in tax-deferred retirement plans such as IRAs, and by purchasing tax-deferred annuities and variable and universal life insurance. Defined contribution pension plans are retirement funds held in trust by the employer for the employees, who bear all the risk of the portfolio. Defined benefit pension plans give the employee a claim to some fixed-amount annuity, with the amount determined by years of service and wage history. The Black/Dewhurst proposal is a strategy by which companies with defined benefit pension plans exploit the tax-exempt status of the plan's assets.

PROBLEMS

1. You are now 25 years old and plan to work until you are 65. You plan to die at 85. Your labor income is $50,000 per year and you expect to get a Social Security benefit of $10,000 per year. Assuming no taxes, no growth in labor income, and a real rate of interest of 3%, how much will real savings be to consume a constant amount for the next 60 years?

2. Answer Problem 1 assuming the real rate is 4%.

3. Answer Problem 1 assuming the Social Security system won't exist in forty years.

4. Consider investing $100,000 in a bond that pays 16% interest versus investing in a stock with a 6% dividend yield and a 10% price appreciation per year. You plan to sell after four years. If you are in the 28% tax bracket, what is the difference in the after-tax strategies?

5. Answer Problem 4 assuming you are in the 34% tax bracket.

SOLUTIONS

1. C = amount consumed per year. The present value of C for 60 years equals the present value of the labor and Social Security income.

    Present value of labor income = $30,000 (PVIF$_A$ 3%, 40 years)
    = $693,443.16

    Present value of Social Security benefits
    = 10,000 (PVIF$_A$ 3%, 20)(PVIF 3%, 40)
    = $45,607.92
    Total present value = 693,443.16 + 45,607.92 = $739,051.08

    739,051.08 = C (PVIF$_A$ 3%, 60)

    C = $26,704.10

2. Present value of labor income = $30,000 (PVIF$_A$ 4%, 40)
   = $593,783.22
   Present value of Social Security benefits
   = 10,000 (PVIF$_A$ 4%, 20)(PVIF 4%, 40)
   = $28,307.16
   Total present value = 593,783.22 + 28,307.16 = $622,090.38

   622,090.38 = C (PVIF$_A$ 4%, 60)

   C = $27,497,54

3. 693,443.16 = C (PVIF$_A$ 3%, 60)

   C = $25,056.15

4. The after tax yield on the bond = .16(.72) = .1152

   After four years you have 100,000 $(1.1152)^4$ = $154,671.76

   The yield after four years to the stock strategy before the capital gains tax is

   100,000 $(1 + .0432 + .10)^4$ = $170,800.39

   The capital gain = 100,000 $(1.10)^4$ - 100,000
   = $46,410

   The tax is .28(46,410) = $12,994.80, so after the capital gains tax the yield is 170,800.39 - 12,994.80 = $157,805.59, which is $3,133.83 greater than the bond strategy yield.

5. After-tax yield on the bond
   = .16(.66) = .1056
   After four years the bond strategy yields

   100,000 $(1.1056)^4$ = $149,414.28

   The yield after four years to the stock strategy before the capital gains tax is
   100,000 $(1 + .0396 + .10)^4$ = $168,659.09

   The capital gain is 46,410 with the capital gains
   tax = .34(46,410) = $15,779.40

   so yield = 168,659.09 - 15,779.40 = $152,879.69
   which is $3465.41 greater than the yield on the bond strategy.